# 1 MONTH OF
# FREE
# READING

## at

## www.ForgottenBooks.com

By purchasing this book you are eligible for one month membership to ForgottenBooks.com, giving you unlimited access to our entire collection of over 1,000,000 titles via our web site and mobile apps.

To claim your free month visit:

www.forgottenbooks.com/free46160

ISBN 978-0-332-20381-2
PIBN 10046160

# The American Boy
## and
# The Social Evil

FROM A PHYSICIAN'S STANDPOINT

BY

## ROBERT N. WILLSON, M.D.

Instructor in Medicine and University Physician,
University of Pennsylvania
Fellow of the College of Physicians of Philadelphia

———

THE JOHN C. WINSTON COMPANY
PHILADELPHIA
CHICAGO          1905          TORONTO

Copyright 1905
By ROBERT N. WILLSON

What is a child?
A man!  The world itself, and
All its possibilities, and hopes, and joys,
And love and hate, and victory, and sorrow!
All that inspires life's war:—
Still sleeping!

# THE WHEREFORE

THE following pages are published in the earnest hope that they may assist in the preservation of the American home circle through their influence upon the boy and the young man.

Each of the four chapters was prepared for those who listened to it, and with no idea that it would eventually find its way into print. I have now arranged them in permanent form for the purpose of more widely introducing a difficult and delicate subject in a plain but thoroughly clean way.

For years I have felt the need, as an individual and a physician, of a simple, and yet scientifically accurate, presentation of the world's great blemish, its causes, and effects, in such a form that I might safely place it in the hands of the American boy and girl. Each of the chapters comprising this little volume has been chosen with this end in view. Each has been utilized, moreover, in response to a desire, expressed openly and often, by men and women who have the integrity of American manhood deeply at heart. That addressed to " the boy himself " formed the basis of a series of informal meetings held, at the request of the Director of Public Health and Charities, with the boys of various sections of the City of Philadelphia during the summer of 1904. The second talk was presented to the students of my own University in the autumn of 1903, and later in the form of a pamphlet found its way among the students of many of the large American universities and colleges, as well as of the government institutions at West Point and Annapolis.

Many letters witnessed the approval of prominent members, as well as of the rank and file, of the American medical profession. Among others was one from a former University of Pennsylvania professor, Dr. William Osler, who wrote; " I wish all the students in the country could have heard it. The colleges should reprint it for distribution."

These encouraging testimonials assured me of the sympathy of the representative members of the profession in a work which has heretofore been undertaken timidly and with little or no confidence of support from any quarter, and determined me to accept a subsequent invitation to address the students of Union Theological Seminary, in New York City, along the same general lines. The final chapters owe their origin to this invitation, and appear in almost the identical form of two addresses delivered in April 1905 upon the Willard Parker Foundation.

In this fashion has been accomplished a duty which both head and heart dictated long ago, but which professional obligations might have prevented had it not been possible to collect and digest the material in just such an occasional way.

My object throughout has been to employ terms and statistics that any boy or girl, man or woman may understand, and which neither sex need avoid on any other ground than that of prudery. That both fathers and mothers approve this course has been amply demonstrated by their attitude toward the pamphlets already in their possession,* most of which have eventually been placed by themselves in the hands of their children. The statistics seem almost incredible to many of those who have lived in the quiet of a pure life. The most startling have been obtained, however, from my own experience in the practice of my profession, from the Census of the United States, or from equally dependable authority, and not a figure has been cited except it has first undergone investigation and proof. The few criticisms that have reached my ears, (and I have sought them), have come from individuals who have either failed to understand the motive and the necessity, or were ignorant as to the facts, or from those who found it inconvenient to listen to the plainness of truth. The majority of these have within the past year taken the trouble to tell me that they believed themselves to have been in the wrong.

* The Social Evil in University Life.

The facts belong to men and women alike, and if used with good sense and judgment will work a revolution in the ranks of the enemies of the American home altar. If they are laid open to the sunlight they can cause no possible harm, and will at least accomplish good by breaking down the wall of false modesty that has for many a year stood between the evil and its cure.

It is with the wish that every boy and girl, and every father and mother in this wide land may be reached in time to prevent the harm that is almost inevitably, but unnecessarily, in store for many, that this little volume is dedicated to the key to the solution of America's moral problem — the American boy!

ROBERT N. WILLSON, JR.

1708 Locust St., Philadelphia, Pa.

# CONTENTS

ERRATA.

On page 80, line 8, read *marital* for *martial*.
On page 102, line 5, read *twenty* for *ten*.
On page 147, line 8, read *a priori* for *a priore*.

# CONTENTS

# I

## THE NOBILITY OF BOYHOOD:* THE BOY'S PART IN LIFE'S PROBLEM

I wish that each of you might hold the magician's horoscope in his hands for just a few minutes at some time between the ages of fifteen and sixteen years.

"Why?" do you ask? Simply because having been a boy, and being still very much of one myself, I wish you and all the fellows — I like the friendship of that word — could see one or two buoys floating on ahead, and a lightship or so in the distance, that might help you guide the ship straight.

"What do I mean?" I will tell you. At fif-

* The above formed the basis of a series of informal talks to the boys of Philadelphia, delivered during the summer of 1904, at the request of the Department of Public Health and Charities.

13

teen or sixteen you, and all boys, are at the most happily careless time you will ever enjoy. Your father and mother see that the table is well spread; your allowance may or may not be that of a rich man's son,— still, large or small, it comes without much trouble on your part. The sun rises and sets, and the storms brew and rumble away into the far distance, without disturbing your balance more seriously than by the delay of a game, or by postponing your schemes for the matter of a few hours.

Even those of you who were born working, as it were, to whom a holiday is an event to be remembered,— even you will never again be quite as free to do as you wish, or as heedless of the restraint of authority. Yours is the boy's age, and it will soon be behind you. This playtime will soon be gone. Another year will bring college, or business, or responsible work of some kind into the horizon. I want to catch your ears for a few moments — while we are still boys.

Those of you who spend your summers in the country have learned to know something about flowers, and some of you have been told that a flower, when full-grown or ripe, has a mission to perform before it dies. It must provide for others of the same kind which shall come after it. You have perhaps seen the pollen dust, and heard how it must be brought from the stamen to a certain portion of the pistil, and that a growth, as fine as cobweb, extends from the speck of pollen down through the delicate tubes of the pistil; and that this fertilization, as it is called, gives the plant power in due time to produce others of its kind. Often the wind carries the pollen dust from the stamen to the pistil. Often insects act in place of the wind, as in the case of the milkweed, a plant that most of you know almost as well as the farmer, who looks on it as a great source of trouble in his fields. It is everywhere! The Jersey boy, and he of the New England coast, and the boy of the West and the South — all know its scaly green seed-pod. Many of you have squeezed the milk from the stem, which you have broken over your fingers, and felt them sticky for hours after. But how many of you know how it comes that the milk-weed keeps on growing from summer to summer? And how many know how the farmer can make headway against it, and keep it from spreading all over his land? It will not do to say that it just happens! Each plant has hundreds, sometimes more than a thousand flowers. Each flower has two seed cases. Think now, how many of the familiar seed-pods we would reasonably expect when the plant matures. And yet there are usually about one half dozen in all!

Let me tell you what takes place. The Master Mind that fashions every flower, and paints every color into the sky at sunset, and the pale blue of the robin's egg, and the green coat of the frog,—has planned a wonderful means, not only of keeping the milkweed alive from year to year, but of making it just so difficult for this to come about that only a few new flowers grow out of the one that you see today, instead of the thousands that we would suppose.

Each blossom from the cluster of the milk-weed is very tiny, and in its centre is the pistil, flat on top and five-sided. Below the pistil is pointed, and at the lower end the two seed cases are fastened, which, if all goes well, may form ripe seed-pods. On each of the five sides of the pistil is a little stigmatic spot ready to receive the pollen, which must touch this before the seed cases can develop. Closely arranged around the pistil are five stamens, each with three wings, one on each edge and one above. The ten wings on the sides join at their edges, and form in this way five slits. The five wings at the top cover the pistil and hide it from sight. On the inner side of each stamen are two little pockets which hold the pollen, which is arranged in tiny masses, pairs of which are linked together by tiny yokes.

In this manner each flower has ten pollen masses yoked together in pairs. These little yokes stick upward and are very useful, as you will see. There is no easy way for the pollen masses to reach the stigmatic spots on the pistil. Even the wind cannot reach them, hidden away as they are beneath the wings. But if you look closely you will find among these helpless stamens, five tiny nectar cups, full of the fluid which the bees love. The bee grasps the flower with her six legs, and empties one after another of the nectar cups. Before she has finished, however, and when she tries to fly away, she finds that her hairy legs have caught in the tiny slits formed by the wings around the stamens, and she keeps moving and pulling and twisting to keep them free. In this way her feet catch in the tiny yokes which hold the pollen masses together, and as the bee flies free, away comes the yoke with the pollen. As it brushes past the pistil it may fertilize the stigmatic spots. Nature does not like this method of inbreeding, as we say when speaking of dogs or cattle, and instead the bee usually flies away with the yokes hanging to her feet until she lights on another flower. Then in trying to empty the nectar cups of this latest flower her feet move around as anxiously as before, the pollen masses of the first touch the stigmatic spots of the new flower, and the work of fertilization is at last well done.

You see how many steps must be gone through

before the milkweed has a chance of new life. The flowers of next season are her children. I could tell you the same story of the dandelion, a flower in whose service over ninety different insects have been found helping to bring the pollen and the fertile spots together. But these things will be interesting for you to study out for yourselves the next time you see a plant or a blossom in the country.

Perhaps some of you knew before I began that the Master Workman has planned each flower, and each plant, and each tree, and each form of animal life, so that as long as it obeys His laws its kind shall not die out. It is so with the milkweed, it is so with the oak, it is just as true of the rose, and the lily, and the ant, and the bee, and the birds, and the fishes, and of all God's creation. This wonderful machinery of Nature is one of the most certain proofs in our possession that the world did not simply grow, and keep on in its busy toil, without an Architect and without a Guide.

And now you say, "If this is true of all that

God has made for man, why do you stop when you have left out His most wonderful creation — man himself?"

It is a fair question, and, like most that come from a boy, it makes us think. "Why?" Because the birth of a baby, and its first thought, the time its eye first rests for a second on the mother, the earliest step of the wobbly little leg, the growth into childhood, and, years after, into the man;— all of this is so wonderful, and so hard for you and me to understand, that I hesitated before I dared to talk of it to you.

Some of you remember that a time came when your mother was hidden away from you for a little time. Then soon you heard the cry of a tiny baby, and your father told you that the stork had visited the home, or that the doctor had brought a baby in his satchel. All you knew or cared to know was that your "nose was broken" for the time, and that the new baby called for a great deal more attention than was its share, or than you had ever required. By and by you saw the little red thing, and wondered why it rolled its eyes around so, and why, when it was not rolling its eyes, it was always crying, and why it so often needed to have its head tucked in close to its mother's breast,— and, strangest of all, why it stopped crying as soon as she put it in that uncomfortable position!

You have learned what many of these things mean by this time. You know, many of you, that God has planned to keep men and women on this earth for a time, provided they obey the laws He has made for them, and provided also — this being very important — that our fathers and mothers obeyed these laws before we were born. We know, and we must never forget, especially the boys, that like the milkweed we are part of His plan, and that we must help Him carry out the world's history, which He cannot make without us.

> He "could not make Antonio Stradivari's violins Without Antonio."

Three things I want to tell you about our part in helping this work on, and all three, remember, come from the heart of one of your older boy friends. The first is this: that each one of you will have a serious part to play in keeping the world alive and healthy, and your work has already begun.

The second: that you will be held responsible, no matter what your age, for every bit of good, as well as for all the unhappiness, or sorrow, or uncleanliness of mind, or body, or disease, that comes into the world through yourself or your children, or by your influence in whatever way.

And the third: that boys and girls have already in their possession a pearl of great price, a treasure that they must not risk losing, since it is a trust from the great Captain, and must be handed back to Him perfect.

Just a word or two about each of these things.

First of all, What part can a boy have to play in keeping God's world in healthy life? Does it matter to the world whether or no one particular boy lives? Do not most people think boys are in the way? I believe not! Most people do not think that boys are a nuisance, though many of them do indeed say so. Was Napoleon's boyhood worth while? Was that of Washington or Lincoln? When you and they stop to consider you will say that it certainly does make a vast difference not only whether the boy lives, but much more that they help him to live well, particularly while he is a boy. This is not only for your own sake.

One day you will see a girl who will come to mean something more to you than the hoyden and tomboy of last summer who could climb the mast, or pull in the sheet rope as readily as you. You even honored her by calling her a " good fellow." High praise this from a boy! But this girl is surely another. She may after all be the same, but what a change has come over both of you since then! You both look much as before, but she is a woman and you a man, and in a few months' time. And soon you will be willing to not only give up your bat and ball, and your boat and fishing tackle, and your gun, but you will even be glad to sit indoors and work over a dreary problem of figures, or stand behind a counter, and by dint of years of effort earn the right to call that woman your wife. And if she is the right kind of a woman she will make you first prove that you are the right kind of a man. With the winning of your wife will begin what God has planned for you, just as for the plant, and the bee, and the bird, and for all men and women,— that you should pass on the life that He has given to you to tiny children, who will be yours, and who will be like you in many ways. Just as you are, so are they likely to be. All things being equal, if your wife and you are healthy and strong in mind and body, your children have every likelihood of inheriting your strength and vigor. You have been made in such a way, and I need not stop to tell how the Master Workman has made you differ in form from woman, in order that the life which He has placed in you may join with the love and life that are in her. In some manner that none of us thoroughly understands He brings a tiny child into the world. Just as the oak must grow from the acorn, and the chick from the egg, and just as the pollen must reach the fertile spot in the milkweed, so God has placed in every woman the earliest thought of a child, and has planned it so that only when the father's life can meet hers, and the two develop together, can the new tiny spirit come into being. Without this power which He has entrusted to you the world must have come to an end long ago. Unless God had trusted your father and mother to treasure the gift He put in their hands, you would not be here. Certain nations appear to be dying out at this very time because they are misusing this power. Some day you will be called on by your Maker to show yourself worthy of his confidence, and to bring to life a son or a daughter who will live after you. That son or daughter should be the ancestor of a long, noble line. The responsibility is the most serious one of your life.

You are wondering now, probably, why I mentioned your accountability for the unhappiness, or sorrow, or disease that you may bring into the world in this way. Is such a thing possible? I shall have to talk plainly to you, and it is because you are almost men that I talk to you at all. You can indeed bring to yourselves not only unhappiness, but sorrow also, and disease, by misuse of this very beautiful privilege that has been given to you. "How," do you ask? Let me say just a word again as an older boy to younger ones. Has any one ever asked you to do, or have you ever known them to do anything which you thought at the time was neither clean nor manly? Has any man or woman or boy or girl ever said anything to you which made you ashamed to look your father or mother in the eye? Have you ever said anything to any boy or girl, or have you ever allowed yourself to do anything that you would be sorry to have known at home or abroad?

There are few boys and few girls that will misunderstand when they are told that God has made them in a particular manner so that later on He can give them the wonderful gift of a child. None of you will misunderstand me, though you may be surprised, when I tell you as a physician that more sickness and disease comes into the world by misuse of this power of the body that has been put in your keeping than in any other way. You may not know that if you trifle with it, or use it wrongly, you may not only gain some serious ailment, but your child, if your wife ever gives you one, will certainly suffer in some way for every harm that comes to you. You ought to be told now, before it is too late, that all of the habits which boys know to be unclean and wrong not only tend to weaken your body, but to destroy your mind and will, and that every one of them helps you to lose the moral strength which you will soon need in order to resist another even more serious temptation. Those of you who have been thrown much with older boys and men already know that many men and women, instead of keeping their bodies sacred until they have found a true mate in life, use them in such a way that a child is often born to unmarried parents who neither wish to have it known that it is their off-spring, nor dare to let the world know their wickedness. Such a child is cursed before it is born! Even its father and mother dare not own it. This thing occurs under God's eyes, as if they thought He could not see, or as if they did not care. It happens in spite of their wish and attempt to prevent it. Still oftener the man or boy takes some foul disease from the woman, or the woman from the man, for neither will long escape mischief in their wrongdoing. All diseases obtained in this way can be and often are passed on to those whom you love, the members of your families and all those around you. Only recently I saw a little baby born with the disease which one of its parents had contracted before marriage. The one that was to blame thought that no harm could come from " just that once "; and there was then no idea of marrying.

Where do we now find ourselves? And what is the reason for this state of affairs?

A boy has perhaps heard someone say that it is manly to do what he knows to be wrong. Out of fear of ridicule or shame this boy ventures to imitate the wrong. There are on the street many women today who spend their lives trying to lead boys such as you into wickedness and mischief. Such women are nearly all (I might safely say all) unclean and diseased, so that it is unsafe for you to touch them. "Why have I told you this?" Because boys are more valuable than grown men. Because I have seen boys no older than you, and boys who were manly in other ways, yield to what they knew to be wrong, because a laugh urged them on. Some of these boys I have helped to get well of the mischief that comes from just such wrongdoing. Will you let me warn you against learning that lesson from bitter experience? Your own harm is sure, but it is the smallest part of the wrong. Though you may not be permanently injured you may still pass the disease, which has laid its grasping hands on you, to someone else. This someone is likely to be your wife or your child, even years after. Is it not horrible to think that it may be anyone, at home or abroad, and you the cause?

And last of all!

You cannot yet know, boys, what a world of pleasure and joy there is in looking down into a baby face, and knowing that part of your life and part of the mother's, and — let us say it with bowed heads — part of God's life, is there. He has given you the greatest of all masteries, that which goes beyond all power of understanding, that power which approaches His own,— the ability and nobility to create life. Will you not keep your minds and bodies clean and pure against the time when He will use you and a pure woman to make her and your fair names live forever in your children.

> "Not God Himself can make man's best
> Without best men to help Him."

# II

## CLEAN LIVING: A PROBLEM OF SCHOOL AND COLLEGE DAYS.*

I CONGRATULATE those of you, today, who are just entering this old University! Those who have already learned to call her **Alma Mater** need no word from me to tell them of the joys and responsibilities of college life. It is because some of us older college boys have learned just what you are to encounter in the four years of city and university experience, that we have called you together for a frank talk on matters that will have a vital influence on your college and after-careers.

You will have guarding over your interests, and watching with a keen and kindly eye your

* A talk with the students of the University of Pennsylvania, October 10, 1903.

successes and failures, one of the warmest-hearted men that our Provost's chair has ever held. In the midst of responsibilities that would bend the shoulders of an ordinary man, you will **find** that he has a smile and a grasp of the hand **for** each one **of you,** no matter how unimportant **you** may consider yourself **to be** in your particular sphere **of** activity. He wishes **you** simply to assure him that **you** are active in that sphere. I have learned to know him as a man whose aim in life **to-day** is the genuine benefit and happiness **of** young **men** like **you** and me.

In close touch with your Provost, and equally a man, **you** will learn to know and love **one of** the best friends of my college days, and **one who** learns **for** the first time to-day, perhaps, that his influence was stronger than almost any other in making my college life of whatever value **to myself** and others it may chance to be. If he could but know how many men have left these walls with the same sentiment in their breasts, he would tell, you, as I now do, that he has not lived in vain. I have seen Vice-Provost Smith, in the midst of his day's work, stop as each of a number of thoughtless students pushed his way into the office, and show the same warm interest in the last one that sent the first away with the feeling that he had talked with a friend and one whom he could trust.

For myself, I can simply say that I have worked among you as one of your University physicians for over three years, and that I have considered my work a rare privilege and a sacred trust. I have learned many things of student life which escaped me while a student myself; and I have learned the value, during these thirteen years of college associations, of the opportunity of looking on many of the problems that will soon come before you. Perhaps they mean more to me because I have seen many of them both from the standpoint of the student and later as your confidential medical friend.

One of these problems involves a temptation that meets every man sooner or later, will certainly meet you during your college days, and perhaps has already stood in the path of some. I refer to the temptation to risk your health of mind and body by illicit intercourse with women, whom you would be unwilling and even horrified to consider of the same order of being as your mothers or your future wives. Every large city swarms with such women, many of whose lives are wrecked by marital infidelity before they begin to prey upon the happiness of other homes.

Shall I tell you in another way why you are gathered here to-day. Last spring a country boy came to Philadelphia for the first time. He was induced by friends to visit a house of ill fame. He was infected by the woman with gonorrhœa, and, though at the time none of the ordinary symptoms appeared, in a day or so his eyes began to smart. Another of his so-called friends advised him in all earnest to wash his eyes in his own urine. He did this at once. Gonorrhœal inflammation developed, probably had developed before the urine made the infection sure, and to-day that country boy is totally blind and for his lifetime.

Your Provost and Vice-Provost have watched

with increasing interest and alarm the influence upon those who have gone before you of the temptations offered by university life in a great city. They have asked me to talk to you to-day of this matter as one of the students' physicians, and therefore one who ought and I am glad to say does, hold intimate and strictly confidential relations with every one of you that cares to use me as an adviser and friend.

In the last three years of my work among the students of this University I have seen you at times, and under conditions, that have led you to open your hearts to me; whether always through friendship or necessity it is at present unnecessary to inquire. I have seen many of you at times when you would have given worlds had some one told you in advance of the facts which I hope to make plain to you to-day. I have listened, more regretfully on each occasion, to the old cry, "Why did not some one tell me in time?" until it seemed impossible that another year should be allowed to slip by without giving those who are coming on the warning of the experience of those who have gone before. I have seen some of you injured physically, and for life, by either the lack of some such frank, clear discussion of the dangers of impure living, or by wilful disregard of advice in the few instances in which it had been offered.

In my capacity as University physician, therefore, and one who holds himself ready to serve you at any time, day or night, I wish to talk briefly but earnestly of three of the most inevitable results of impure sexual life. I have said that the opportunity of lowering yourselves in the eyes of God and of true men will certainly be presented to you within the nearest future. In a large city this is unfortunately and peculiarly true. Example, fear of ridicule, or curiosity may be the impelling force; and if any one influence has had a dastardly effect upon the lives of young men, ridicule is that one. Whatever or whoever you are, we are interested in you, and want you to know to-day and finally that you transgress the laws of pure sexual living at your peril, and perhaps literally, sooner or later, at the cost of your life.

# CLEAN LIVING

It may be stated with the barest possibility of error that no man who has once had sexual intercourse with a woman not his wife, fails to make a habit of the crime. It is equally certain that no one has indulged in such excesses without sooner or later contracting some venereal disease. This is so literally true that such conditions are considered among medical men as inevitable attendants upon impure intercourse with the other sex. Every preventive has been tried, and all have failed. On the other hand, let me say to you as a physician voicing the consensus of medical opinion, that there has never existed a man who could not live a healthy, active existence, throughout his whole life, in the absence of any sexual intercourse whatsoever. It is a common story among college students that after a certain age a man requires sexual satisfaction, if he is to preserve vigor of mind and body. Let me characterize this idea as a curse that has done more harm in the home-world than any other influence, and one which, together with ignorance of the inevitable results in the way of venereal infection, has made it unsafe for men and women to drink out of a neighbor's glass, or for men to accept a pipe or a cigar or a cigarette from the fingers of a friend unless they know him through and through in a way that few men are known. Nature has provided for man's sexual necessities in a way with regard to which you do not need to be informed, and that provision is one that is as ample as it is providential. If, in addition, a boy has a wise father, who remembers his own temptations and takes a judicious and the only fair way of strengthening his son against them, by opening his eyes to the danger of transgressing Nature's laws, he is well equipped for growth into noble and healthy manhood. Would that every boy had such a father! Too often the whole subject is treated in open conversation as a necessary and unavoidable evil. We should look upon the man or woman who trifles with the subject of sexual impurity as a criminal, either by virtue of ignorance or by intent, and we will even then not reward them as they deserve. We have come to a time when, if the young men of this and other countries do not engage and conquer the social evil, it must be accomplished by the enlightenment of the pure women that still exist; and when your mothers and your future wives and your daughters are warned even against their sons, husbands, and fathers, because they are dangers to humanity, you will begin to regret that you did not lay hold on the cause in time. The trend of the law is in this direction, and by the nature of things it is bound to insist upon it sooner or later. Lincoln is said to have made the remark that " every man who contemplated marriage should stand over the doctor with a club and make him tell the truth in reference to the chosen partner for life. Also that the parents who would allow a girl to marry a man without knowing as clearly as could be known his physical as well as his moral condition deserved to be scalped."

Unfortunately, no one is in a position as yet to know these things certainly, and no woman will believe them of her lover. Yet men have married women the day after lying with a common prostitute, and days and perhaps weeks and months after syphilis or gonorrhœa has appeared in the man, who invariably has been ignorant or cowardly enough to transmit the disease to his wife rather than acknowledge his condition. Many another man has struggled for months towards a cure and has been pronounced well by his physician, only to infect his wife with his latent disease. Add to this the fact that the average physician is unqualified to treat gonorrhœa and syphilis successfully, and should not attempt the task, and you will learn how helpless the victim of such a disease is. In all this great city there is hardly a hospital bed that will admit openly and as such a subject of venereal disease. There is a tremendous duty to-day upon the physician and parents to learn and disseminate the truth in regard to sexual sin, and my conscience will be clearer when I have spoken to you.

Let me talk to you of three conditions, gonorrhœa, syphilis, and illegitimate fatherhood, the three most frequent attendants upon harlotry, and the two former of which are far more contagious and widespread than tuberculosis, which is occu-

pying the attention of the public to-day. At the
end of our discussion I trust I may have proved
assertions which may seem to you at first harsh
and extreme.

## GONORRHŒA.

It may be a significant fact to you that the first
student treated by me after my appointment as
students' physician and the last one seen at the
close of the session of 1902-3, were suffering
from gonorrhœa contracted during illicit intercourse with a woman. Both of these were sons of
refined, well-to-do fathers and mothers. Both of
them were ignorant of the imminent danger of infection, and both quoted the oft-heard lie, that " a
case of gonorrhœa is no worse than a bad cold."
Both men had been told this lie by other students,
who had themselves previously contracted and
suffered from the disease. One had repeated at-
tacks before consulting me, and was then in a
serious condition. One of these students is apparently well to-day. The former will carry
traces of his gonorrhœa to his grave, and can

never be the father of a child. He should certainly never marry, both for this reason and for fear of infecting his wife.

During the three intervening years between these two cases, a number of students have consulted me each month, and many with the same story of ignorance of danger. All knew, no doubt, but few realized the fact until too late. Some few, through despair of being cured of a chronic condition, had thrown precaution to the winds and contracted new infection and new trouble. In one instance that came under my care a woman, herself a medical student at another institution, had infected five men with gonorrhœa, and one of them either she or some other had also infected with syphilis. Two of these men were brothers, yet it would appear that none of the five had confided in any of the rest.

It seems strange that it should not be generally known by students that there is little likelihood of a woman who admits of such attentions herself escaping venereal infection, no matter what her social status or what her precautions. It is a rule borne out by medical experience that a woman who encourages the advances of one man will invariably entertain others. It is also a frequent experience for a number of men separately to consult a physician and assure him that the subject of their attention could not possibly have infected them, as she had never had intercourse with any other man, and yet the fact appear clear to the physician that she had infected each and every one. It is safe to say that every harlot (I use this term advisedly, with reference to her of good family connections, for there are such, as well as to the common prostitute; they belong in the same category) has at some time been infected with gonorrhœa, and if one stops to learn how difficult and rare a thing it is to thoroughly cure a woman of gonorrhœa, he will understand also how dangerous it is to trust himself at any time in her subsequent life within her infected presence.

A few statistics may serve as an illustration, not only of the prevalence of temptation on the streets of a great city, but of the ubiquity of gonorrhœal disease in its many forms. It has been well characterized as the most widespread of all contagious diseases, with the single exception of measles. It has been shown that in some of the cities of Europe more than one-half of the entire population, and more than three-quarters of the male population, suffer from gonorrhœal infection. Dr. Allen reports from one hospital dispensary in New York City 86,000 cases of all kinds treated in 1900, of which over 3,000 were cases of venereal disease. In 1903 we learn from a commission appointed to study the subject that there are in New York City to-day about 200,000 syphilitic subjects, and probably four times as many (800,000) cases of gonorrhœa. To care for these cases and to prevent the spread of infection, there is one bed for every 5,000. This ratio holds good for nearly all the large cities of America. While all prostitutes are considered gonorrhœic subjects, it is estimated that every fourth one is qualified to transmit syphilis.

In Prussia it is estimated that there are annually 773,000 cases of venereal disease. Still more exact are the following figures. Out of 1,155 patients (mostly venereal) treated at Hot Springs, Arkansas, and coming from all over the United States, it was learned that 818 (70 per cent.) had, at the time of examination, or had had, gonorrhœa; 337 had never contracted the infection. Most of these patients were from the so-called better classes. The ages at which the gonorrhœa was contracted varied from 10 to 57 years, averaging 21.8 years. Three hundred and eighty-two cases were below 21 years of age and 58 cases were below 17 years. Of 60,000 sick soldiers in our army of occupation in the Philippines, 10,000 were cases of venereal disease; nearly all of these have since come home, and many remain uncured to-day.

These figures will suffice to show that gonorrhœa is so frequent a condition that it literally leaves few homes unscathed, if the truth be fully known. As already stated, the prostitute offers a ready infection to the male urethra in its virgin state, and a still more likely one to a chronically inflamed mucous membrane. Probably she can and does infect as long as she lives, and undoubtedly she does infect many men in one day. Long after she is visibly cured she may be a source of virulent infection. The result is that she may be honest in believing herself free from danger to others and become the more dangerous in the belief of her cure. Under the most benign circumstances she is a danger, and under the worst she is a scourge. Infected many times, with each new occasion she becomes freshly virulent. The result is that the world is to-day overrun with venereal disease. Let me ask a few questions that naturally arise, and in their answers endeavor to emphasize the points I wish to bring home to you.

*What is gonorrhœa in the male subject?* An extremely infectious disease, usually involving some portion or all of the urinary passage from the bladder outward. Any portion of the body may, however, be infected, including the eyes, the skin, the nose, ears, mouth, bowel, and any or all of the internal organs of the body. Its minimum average duration is six weeks. It often lasts for years, and unless promptly and intelligently treated its effects often remain evident for life. It is a disease for which eminent specialists are constantly seeking some new and effective remedy, *which has not yet been found.* The question is still under discussion whether either syphilis or gonorrhœa is certainly curable. One prominent student of the subject says of the latter, "I have studied and treated gonorrhœa for fifteen years, and I feel to-day that I know less about that disease than I thought I did several years ago." Another writes, " A large number of chronic gonorrhœas, speaking generally, remain uncured. Some of these may be explained by the indolence and discouragement of the patient, others by want of care or understanding on the part of the physician, others by constant reinfection, and still others from no tangible cause, all gonococci having 'apparently' been eliminated." Still another says, " The importance of gonorrhœa with that of syphilis is 100 to 1, not only from the standpoint of the number of persons attacked, but also from the standpoint of the gravity of the lesions and their perpetuity."

Have I said enough to prove to you that gonorrhœa is " worse than a bad cold?"

*What are its possible complications and their frequency?* Among the most frequent of the complications of gonorrhœa are stricture of the urinary passages and sometimes even of the bowel, inflammation and destruction of the internal genital apparatus (the testicles and the tubes leading thereto), blindness, bladder and kidney disease, abscess at any point in the body, and joint rheumatism — all frequent conditions. Less frequent are septic blood infection (usually fatal), brain disease, degeneration of the spinal cord, heart disease, bone disease, peritonitis, pneumonia, and death. You may ask, " Why have we not heard before of the serious features of what we believed to be a temporary inflammation?" I answer, " Because every case of gonorrhœal infection is concealed more jealously than a crime would be, and if serious complications follow, the specific origin is denied or withheld by both the victim and his doctor." Last winter an officer of the University showed his interest in one of the students by calling on him in the University Hospital. He was told by the student and by the nurse that the trouble was appendicitis, and was shocked and disheartened later on when he learned that the case was one of gonorrhœa.

A large percentage of cases of chronic gonorrhœa leave behind a stricture of the urethra. Nearly all leave an irritable and often a diseased prostate gland; many leave an irritable or diseased bladder.

Between 10 and 20 per cent. of all cases of infantile blindness are due to gonorrhœal infection. Statistics of the German Empire for 1894 showed that 80 per cent. of all children born with healthy eyes who became blind did so as the result of transmitted gonorrhœa. In that country there are 30,000 cases of blindness to-day due to gonorrhœa, and mostly transmitted from other persons. In spite of all the latest knowledge and the newest methods, approximately 600 cases of blindness occur annually in Germany from this one avoidable cause. In this country from 25 to 50 per cent. of the blind in institutions owe their loss of sight to gonorrhœal infection. In one year in New York City 136 cases of gonorrhœal ophthalmia were reported.

Inflammation of the epididymus (the tube from the testicle outward) is a very frequent complication, often resulting in absolute sterility, as will be shown later.

Gonorrhœal rheumatism is also a serious affection, usually occurring in a large joint like the hip or knee, and frequently leaving a permanent disability.

The other complications mentioned occur with varying frequency, depending upon the attention paid to the condition by doctor and patient, as well as upon the promptness with which the disease yields to treatment. While far less frequent, they are even more serious. There is no question that many cases of kidney disease owe their origin to gonorrhœa, many resulting years after in fatality. During each year a number of deaths are recorded as directly due to infection by the gonococcus of one of the vital organs of the body. While writing this statement, I have before me the records of five fatal cases that have come easily to my notice, three from gonorrhœal peritonitis, one from gonorrhœal valvular disease of the heart, and one of gonorrhœal septicæmia, which will be mentioned later.

*Can gonorrhœa be cured, and can the patient be sure he is cured?* To the first question probably " yes," and to the second certainly " no." We have already heard doubtful statements of eminent students of the disease. Neisser, one of the first authorities of the world on venereal disease, claims that gonorrhœa can be cured. Your own professors of surgery, White and Martin, also claim that it can. All admit that very many cases are not cured, owing to one reason and another. Every year brings forward new instances of old, supposedly cured infection relighted by disease, debility, or debauch. In children, undoubtedly, the prognosis is better than in adults, probably because the disease is taken in hand earlier and more systematically; also because all the tissues in the child tend towards healthy growth. Frank, in Germany, has shown, however, that the gonococcus may remain quiescent in the prostate gland for months and years. No symptoms remain, yet the disease may be re-lighted and others be infected.

I have already quoted van der Poel to the effect that a large number of chronic gonorrhœas remain uncured. Köppen cites many cases in which all symptoms had disappeared, and yet the disease remained latent. In regard to one of these he says, " Not one sign was left of a previous gonorrhœa." Six years later there was irritation of the urethra, and he obtained gonococci from the urinary canal. In another case none of the germs of gonorrhœa had ever been discovered in the discharge, though the clinical picture was complete. Six years later he found gonococci in the urethra. He concludes his article with the statement, " Gonococci can exist for years in the organism, as proved by numberless cases." A case is described in one of our own medical journals, dated September, 1903, in which a man infected his own eye with gonorrhœa after six years, during which the disease appeared to be cured. At the same time all his joints became involved, as well as the tendon sheaths of one foot. The gonococcus was obtained from the discharges of the eye, proving the real nature of the infection.

Our answer to the question, then, must be, that under favorable circumstances gonorrhœa probably can be cured. No case is cured until all gonococci have disappeared from the urethra. Many doctors either do not know how or do not take the trouble to look for these micro-organisms. Many patients never return for completion of the cure after the symptoms have become tolerable. Under the best treatment, it should be remembered, success may not be attained. Only time will show whether an actual and permanent cure has been secured. No victim of gonorrhœa can be absolutely sure, when the symptoms have disappeared, that he is cured of his infection, or that he will not infect his wife years after.

*How long after an attack can a man infect a woman with gonorrhœa?* We have already seen in our answer to the preceding question that years may pass by and a man may still be infectious to a wife. As long as there are active symptoms, transmission of the disease is likely. When these have subsided the danger decreases, but never disappears until the last gonococcus has been destroyed. If gonococci can live six, ten, and fifteen years in the organs of the body, as they have been shown to do, probably they can live longer and to an almost indefinite time. The only inference from the cases cited is that the gonorrhœic subject must never be surprised if he finds in after years that his disease has remained latent, and that he has infected some innocent person. The possibility is always before him.

*What are the possible permanent injuries from an attack of gonorrhœa?* We will at present consider only the male sex. It has already been shown that fatality is occasional. The most frequent permanent disability is a chronic gleet or catarrh of the urethra, prostate gland, the bladder, or of all three. Such a chronic inflammation of the urethra usually results in stricture of that passage. Stricture causes obstruction to the flow of urine, and as a consequence bladder inflammation often follows, and the disease often spreads from there to the kidney by direct extension. Gonorrhœal rheumatism very frequently — we may say nearly always — leaves a crippled joint.

By far the most serious sequela of gonorrhœa is sterility, or lack of power to produce progeny. The commission appointed by the American Medical Association estimated that 42 per cent. of all gonorrhœic subjects become sterile, and that many more cause sterile marriages after the first childbirth because of the infection and consequent sterility of the wife. Czerny says that " 50 per cent. of all sterility is due to the husband's gonorrhœa." Morrow says, " Syphilis curses the child; gonorrhœa prevents its existence by rendering the male sterile."

President Roosevelt has recently spoken of the social evil, meaning the wilful sterility of the wedded life. Would that he might cry out from his Presidential chair against the dangers of venereal infection and the real cause of sterility of the sons of **America**.

*What are the results of gonorrhœa in the woman?* Fewer women, by far, are cured of gonorrhœa than is the case with man. I shall not speak, however, of the clinical picture in the female sex. It will be sufficient to say that with the woman gonorrhœa means almost certainly an infection of her internal organs, and sooner or later a serious operation. Pregnancy increases the danger of upward and general infection. Sometimes there is no serious sign of trouble until the woman becomes pregnant. Nöggerath states that 50 per cent. of sterile women owe their sterility to gonorrhœa. Neisser, already quoted, fixes the percentage at a higher figure. Ascher found that of 227 sterile women in his care, 121 were sterile owing to gonorrhœa.

Sänger says that abortion occurs as frequently owing to gonorrhœa as it does as the result of syphilis. Nöggerath cites the cases of 53 women, pregnant during a gonorrhœa, of whom 19 aborted. Fruhingsholtz cites 101 cases, of which 23 aborted and 7 went into premature labor. Price, of this city, says that of 1,000 abdominal operations in women 95 per cent. were the result of conditions due to gonorrhœa.

The statistics of the German Empire for 1894 showed that 80 per cent. of the women who died of uterine or ovarian disease died as the result of conditions dependent upon gonorrhœa.

Have I convinced you that the disease is of more significance than a "bad cold?" If not, let me add a final argument; and if you resist the plea of the children, no influence on earth can save you from an experience which you dearly earn.

*Can gonorrhœa be transmitted to others than your wife?* From what I have already told you, you now know that the vast number of cases of gonorrhœa in the woman in married life are instances of innocent infection on her part. We have omitted until now the possibility of infecting others, and by means other than by sexual intercourse. First, and least important by all odds, you can infect your own eyes, nose, mouth or bowel, and probably will unless you learn the virulence of the gonorrhœal germ. Next, you can infect, and usually do infect, the bedclothes, towels, napkins, handkerchiefs, knives, forks, your pipe, and all articles of ordinary and constant use; and sometimes, by means of them, your wife and children, your friends — even, mayhap, your mother. It is the result of nature's protecting laws and not your care that you fail to pass to all who are around you the curse that you have brought upon yourself. Let me prove this to you in all its hideousness of truth. Cook has reported recently a case of a 4-year-old daughter of a 35-year-old father, from a refined family. The father contracted gonorrhœa in the usual manner, and soon the little girl developed the disease. There was absolutely no other traceable source of the infection. Morrow cites the case of a little girl into whose eye a playmate's finger had been poked. The injured child suffered a typical gonorrhœal conjunctivitis, from the discharge of which the gonococci were obtained. Not long ago there was an epidemic of gonorrhœa among the children of Posen in Germany. In two weeks 236 children contracted the disease, which was finally traced to the use of the public bath. Some one had infected the pool. In spite of the constant suppression of such cases, there are many such reported in the medical journals. I have myself seen, in hospital work, many cases of gonorrhœa in children under 5 years, sometimes transmitted by accident, sometimes by intention. Only when the law imposes fine and imprisonment upon him who knowingly infects another person will this crime be blotted out; it may be that a sterner penalty still might be effective (as already suggested), and meted out at the hand of the surgeon's knife.

Innocent infection of children occurs usually among those who sleep in bed with their parents or use the same towels or table linen. Nightclothes, bed linen, towels, sponges, underclothing, soap, the water closet, if once infected, may retain the germs for weeks and months, and the origin of the infection may, sad to say, never be discovered. On the Scandinavian Peninsula every case of venereal infection is reported to the authorities, as it will be some day here. There will then be fewer cases of venereal disease and fewer innocent victims. I believe, moreover, that in this procedure lies the remedy for marital infidelity and for sexual sin in all its forms.

There is another serious phase to the gonorrhœa of children. When once infected they also transmit the disease, and oftentimes in the same manner as their fathers, and with equal avidity. Wolbarst, in New York City, cites 22 cases occurring in his work during two years, in children between 18 months and 12 years of age. The usual mode of infection was attempted sexual intercourse. On investigation he found that it was by no means an unusual occurrence in this district for children not yet in puberty to indulge in sexual intercourse. He saw three cases of boys, 4, 10, and 12 years respectively, infected by girls between 10 and 12 years. Many other cases were due to the child sleeping with parents, brothers, sisters, who had gonorrhœa. Cotton calls attention to a " string of little girls coming to my clinic suffering from gonorrhœa. **A week later,**" he says, " my assistant brought a boy of 10 years who had been infecting these little girls." Last year I saw more than one student of this University who would not return home for his holiday when he heard that he must be careful not to infect himself or his family. I shall never forget the expression of one who said, " God! You don't mean that I might give this to my mother ! "

Boys, forget yourselves ! If you owe anything to that mother, sister, perhaps some day a wife, your children, your friends, servants, even the laundry-woman, do not risk this disease!

Just a word as to *the mortality of gonorrhœa!* This is occasional, though by no means as high as that of syphilis. Only last year there came to my notice the case of a young man, dying from a diffuse abscess and pyæmia (blood-poisoning) of unknown cause. His life was pledged to a lovely girl, who nursed him on the edge of his grave. Both were of our nation's best blood. Cultures from the pus of his abscess and from his blood showed colonies of the gonococcus, and a history of an almost forgotten attack of gonorrhœa was obtained. It is almost too horrible to think of the crime of the future had he lived to marry the woman who was nursing him in an ignorance of the cause of their double sorrow as complete as his own.

Such a tragedy is being enacted certainly many times every year in this wide world, and bids fair to become an even more frequent occurrence. I have mentioned four other deaths to you. The aggregate of deaths from the sequelæ and complications of gonorrhœa would amount to no small total, and must soon attract the attention of those who have heretofore looked on it as a passing ailment. Have I made plain to you that as the result of one rash act —

*Your wife* may be a lifelong victim; may be deprived of the power of conception; may lose her life by an operation or by infection?

*Your child* may lose its chance of birth; may, if born, be deprived of sight or hearing; may, if a male, suffer consequences equal to your own; if a female, suffer like the mother?

*Yourself* may never be cured; may infect those who are dearest to you; may lose your own life and waste those of others?

**Let** us now for a brief moment consider syphilis.

## SYPHILIS.

Probably far less need be said about this disease, as its name is known to most of you, and few speak of it lightly. When you learn that many of those who surround you in your daily life are virulent with this disease, and that changeling children are born into our best families as the result of it, and that prostitution is likely to fix the unyielding grasp of syphilis upon you, the knowledge may act as a persuasive to keep you true to your ideals.

*What is syphilis?* It is an infectious disease of the whole system, usually making itself first known by means of what is called a chancre, or initial sore. This is followed usually by a general skin eruption, swelling of the glands, falling of the hair on all parts of the body, and later on by serious disease of the blood-vessels and internal organs. It is usually contracted during sexual intercourse, in the case of men usually in prostitution, in the case of women very frequently in an innocent manner and in wedlock. It involves a course of treatment of at least three years, and sometimes resists all treatment. It is found in the highest and lowest classes of society.

*How prevalent is the disease?* Fournier states that one-seventh of the population of Paris is syphilitic, while in Russia whole towns have been decimated by the disease. The victims in the latter country are mainly women and children, and many cases are due to the kissing of sacred images and to the embraces of syphilitic acquaintances. In certain of the European countries 25 per cent. of the population of some of the villages is syphilitic, in most instances due to innocent infection, prostitution being almost unknown. China and Japan are overrun with syphilis. It has been estimated ("Dictionary of Statistics," Mulhall) from the cases in the military hospitals in Europe

that between 7 and 43 per cent. of the entire sol-
diery is infected; the average national percentage
was found to be 14 per cent. The report of the
American Dermatological Society finds that 11.5
per cent. of all skin diseases are syphilitic. And
in our own country again. Out of 1,485 cases
(mostly venereal) treated and questioned at Hot
Springs, Arkansas, in 1901, 831 had had syphilis.
Gihon estimates that there are 2,000,000 cases of
the disease constantly in the United States.

Sänger has shown that nearly one-half of all
the prostitutes in New York City freely admit
that they have had syphilis, and half of these give
birth to syphilitic children. And as a gloomy
shroud for all these figures, Morrow finds that 70
per cent. of the syphilis in the women of New
York City is the result of conjugal infidelity.

*Can syphilis be cured?* This is a far more
difficult question to answer than that with regard
to gonorrhœa. My personal belief is that it usually can, if well treated and in time. A cure,
under the most favorable circumstances, requires
at least three years of constant medication. Many

cases require a longer time. Some prominent syphilologists declare that the disease is incurable. Certain cases are absolutely incurable. Among these may be cited one reported recently by Schamberg, which was under treatment without success for eight years; also two malignant cases reported by Fournier in 1899. The general prognosis of syphilis is probably a good one. The constant danger that the treatment has not been sufficiently radical or thorough always threatens, however, and is well expressed by Osler when he speaks of "the extraordinary frequency of the cerebral and other complications in persons who have had the disease, and who may even have undergone thorough treatment." Howard has reported a case seemingly cured and relighted, after a year of quiescence, by influenza. Many other cases appear to be free from symptoms for a time and then die of insanity, softening of the brain, locomotor ataxia, or some other nervous disease.

*How long after infection can the disease be transmitted to others?* During the entire period of what are called the primary and secondary stages. The latter, if the disease has been thoroughly and conscientiously treated, is usually confined to the first few years following the infection. Only in exceedingly rare instances has infection taken place after the fifth or sixth year. Such cases do, however, occur. Sack reported last year the case of a man on whose person appeared an ulcer (gummatous) ten years after the original attack, and infected his young wife, who displayed typical symptoms of a new syphilitic infection. Six months later she also had a miscarriage. Herscher reports a case of contagion from a husband who unquestionably contracted the disease thirteen years previously. Kopelinski has reported two cases of inherited syphilis infecting previously healthy individuals, and (an almost unheard-of thing) in both instances a grandmother.

*What are the effects of syphilitic infection upon the man?* Perhaps the most serious is the fact that he becomes at once a source of danger to his family, friends, and society in general. This begets the next most serious influence, which is the mental condition. Fournier cites 18 cases of suicide in young syphilitics. We have already sketched the course of the disease itself, and need not repeat the symptoms here. Probably the most serious physical damage is done the blood-vessels and kidneys. Many a case of apoplexy and aneurism is directly due to syphilitic change in the arteries of the brain or elsewhere. Many cases of insanity are also due to this disease. At present there is an attempt to prove what many authorities believe to be true, that locomotor ataxia is purely and simply a syphilitic picture. Many cases of syphilis become and remain completely bald, with no eyebrows and no facial hair. Some few severe cases lose all the bony features of the face, the nose and roof of the mouth undergoing complete necrosis (bone gangrene). Many have a persistent skin eruption. Those who inherit syphilis are usually marked for life and die at an early age. Tuberculosis frequently accompanies or follows syphilis, like the driver of a hearse.

*What are the effects of syphilis upon the*

*woman?* The physical effects are the same as those in the man. If she bears children during the course of the disease, they are likely to be syphilitic and otherwise defective. Still more likely will they be still-born or abortion take place. There is no other cause of abortion that compares with the vicious influence of this disease.

A syphilitic woman is likely to infect many more persons than a man. If a prostitute, she probably infects most of those with whom she has intercourse. Even in every-day life, a syphilitic woman is a source of great danger. Kissing is the most prolific source of transmission next to sexual congress, and especially in this country, where men confine their embraces to their intimates only and to the female sex, unless it be in the case of children. A woman's embraces are much more promiscuous, and she proves much the more active in spreading the disease.

*What are the effects of syphilis upon the offspring?* These are two, and both are serious in the extreme. First, a tremendous percentage of the children born of syphilitic parentage are deficient mentally and physically. Secondly, between 20 and 40 per cent. of all conceptions by a syphilitic woman result in either abortion, still-birth, or premature labor. Even if born with a competent mind, the child who has inherited syph-ilis is cursed as Job was not. It is likely to die before it reaches puberty, and is generally marked so as to be an object of pity throughout its life, to itself as well as to those who know the cause.

*How can syphilis be transmitted?* By contact with a syphilitic sore during the primary and secondary stages of the disease, also with the blood, with the saliva, or any fluid that may carry with it the discharges from a mucous patch or other syphilitic lesion, etc., etc. Usually the in-fection is transmitted during sexual intercourse, though extragenital and innocent infections are now recognized to be very frequent, as by means of knives, forks, spoons, drinking glasses, pipes, cigars, etc., etc. Kissing, as has already been stated, is one of the most frequent methods of contagion. There is danger in any abraded sur-face upon the body when in company with a syphilitic in the infectious stages of the disease. A mother may infect a baby, a baby may infect a nurse, the father may infect the whole family. Weitlander has reported within the last three weeks two instances of infection of entire families, in each case by a small child, known to be syphilitic, who was taken in to board. The infection undoubtedly took place by means of spoons, dishes, etc. If any warning given at this time will take root in the minds of those who are unfortunate enough to have contracted the disease innocently, and to have extragenital sores upon their body, it must be this, that such cases are the most dangerous to mankind. The very irony of this fact makes it the more pitiful, and the crime of the original infection the greater. I do not think I need emphasize the burden of the cry of the infected one, who would warn each one of you from the possibility of becoming a danger to your family, your doctor, and all around you.

*What is the mortality of syphilis?* In England, in the period 1880–90, 1,742 males over five years of age died from the disease. Whole towns have been decimated in Russia. Last year in Philadelphia there were 37 deaths registered as due directly to syphilis. If we add the many deaths due to apoplexy directly dependent upon syphilitic arteries, or to other more obscure syphilitic conditions, the total would in all likelihood be an appalling one. It is sufficient to say that there is a decided mortality as the direct result of the disease and its complications that cannot be overlooked. The secondary mortality has recently been brought home in a most impressive way by Fournier, a French physician, already quoted, who has collected 18 cases of suicide directly or indirectly dependent upon the knowledge of the patient that he had syphilis.

### ILLEGITIMATE FATHERHOOD.

There is only one condition more serious than those of which we have been speaking, to which the man subjects himself who trifles with his power of reproducing the image of his Maker. This is the risk that he runs of impregnating the woman with whom he has sexual intercourse.

Except in the rarest instances, she knows her danger, and endeavors to provide for it. I trust it is true that few men realize until it is too late, how often the precautions of their mistresses fail. Probably no woman exists, of normal development, who, having made a practice of illicit sexual intercourse, has failed to conceive, and to be delivered of the product of conception. Usually the delivering is premature (under the direction, I believe, of a merciful Creator) and the life of the fetus dies out with its birth. Often, however, a child is born into the world, whose father and mother will not, and dare not, own it, and who look upon its life as a cloud upon their future, and a menace against their reputation (fair now only in name) to be dissipated not even when the grave closes over them. The illegitimate may still trace its inheritance to the dead parent who refused, when alive, to acknowledge his title of fatherhood.

If the mother conceives, the father is responsible for the life, whether the child is born to live, or whether it dies in the womb. If murder can be forgotten, and if it rests lightly on the soul of any man, he who fathers an illegitimate child has this one recourse. Even the law holds the crime to be murder after the child is viable. The moral law, which upholds the only true standard of right, declares murder to begin when the living product of conception is destroyed. Here, then, is a danger compared with which gonorrhœa and syphilis are trifling peccadilloes, and in the knowledge of which the human race should hide its face in shame. In Europe and in America whole institutions are populated by children, without father or mother, the harvest of crime. Do you dare to swell the number of that army of children, who will one day claim their unworthy parents before a higher Tribunal than public opinion or human law?

Let us now gather together the lines of our talk. I have told you many of the consequences of gonorrhœal disease. I have purposely said much less of syphilis. Other venereal infections I have entirely passed by. I have told you that prostitution means possible criminal fatherhood. May I now fairly ask you for your decision in regard to certain questions which I put to you earlier in the day? Is prostitution worth while? Is it safe? Do you dare to run the risk? Have I said enough to sufficiently warn without rendering you callous through overtalking? If so, I shall welcome the day when your Provost asked me to work among you as students' physician.

There are those who make light of the social crime, and you now know why I shudder when I hear them trifle about a subject of the gravity of which they know nothing. I have recently read a book by one of the prominent literary women of the day, as full of vile insinuation, and as wicked in its flagrant discussion of man's and woman's infidelity, as if she had never heard of a wrecked home or life. The story itself was of a social crime, and was read with avidity by the unthinking public. Perhaps you have all read it.

This very summer there appeared a book which I found on my library table, loaned by a " friend " to my wife. Its central figures were separated by the crime of the age and, though lovers indeed, could not marry. There were three other marriages prominently introduced into the story, and two of these were blighted by infidelity of one or the other party. I read this book because the author — this time a man — had written others of surpassing beauty and brilliancy of thought and theme. If such books influence others as they do me, their authors must shoulder many a responsibility for a mental and moral downward plunge, and only after an effort a struggle upward. God forgive any one, I say, who dares urge a man, and, above all, a young unmarried man, to trifle with the purity of sexual relations as these writers have presumed to do!

And now one last word to a body of men that will one day take part in the destiny of this country. I have carefully avoided telling you that you owe the sterling purity of mind, soul, and body to your God and Maker. I trust that some one else may do this in the near future and in this same old chapel, whose benches already hold the sons of fathers who have gone before. I would not have you forget the fact that God has made for your use a body that is more wonderful and delicate in its mechanism than any invention of human genius, and that in your power of raising up children after you who may do Him honor He has given you control of a mystery that no scientist has been permitted to unfold. Use this gift nobly and well, and in order to do this thing, guard your purity of thought and action as jealously as you would on the day that you bind yourself, for life and death, to the wife whom God gives you in the place of your mother. You owe to her and to your children a perfect moral and physical legacy!

# III

# THE SOCIAL EVIL
# IN AMERICA.*

I T IS with a sense of high honor that I speak to
you as a fellow student of the Seventh Commandment in its direct relationship to you and me
as consulting physicians in the welfare of the soul
and body.   It is peculiarly fitting that the command " Thou shalt not commit adultery " should
excite an absorbing interest in your calling and
mine, because if we had done and were doing our
full duty its law would not in Christian America
have so far lost its significance and meaning.
Its almost unrestrained violation at the present
day lays the Christian pastor and the Christian
physician open to the charge that certain depart-

* Address to the students of Union Theological Seminary, April
7, 1905.

ments indispensable to our life's business have been seriously and conspicuously neglected, while our effort has elsewhere often been correspondingly misspent. Its vital principle is involved in all forms of illicit sexual indulgence in the single as well as the married state, in libertinism and in the divorce. Indeed, the young man should hold the years preparatory to ~~martial~~ marital life as sacred and responsible as those which follow, and as already the property of not only himself, but of his future life-partner.

If the whole tale were told the physician must shoulder no small share of the moral responsibility for the prevalence of libertinism in America, whether we mean by this term that form permitted and sanctioned in high life by the divorce court, or, among both high and lowly, the crime of the brothel. The physician at least has a thorough knowledge of the consequences of both forms of immorality as shown in retrograde and degenerate processes in the human economy. From such a mother-influence and environment sprang the famous family of Jukes in New York

City, one vicious couple with 1,200 direct de-
scendants or offspring, all traced, of whom 300
died in infancy, 300 were paupers, 7 murderers,
50 prostitutes, 60 thieves, 130 general criminals,
400 early physical wrecks, and many imbecile or
insane.

It hardly required the training of a physician
to recognize the pathologic process involving the
mind of the public when one of your distinguished
fellow citizens dared to write in a current maga-
zine (the " Arena " of February last) the following: " To deny (divorced) persons the right of
remarriage is but an indirect attempt at legalizing compulsory sex-suppression." He failed to
inform you that it is even more true, in most instances, that to allow remarriage after divorce,
whatever the cause, is a very direct attempt at
legalizing adultery in one of its most insidious
forms; though he betrays himself in his conclusion, " So then let us unite to defend the liberty
of all who live natural and happy lives, through
easy divorce and the right of remarriage."

He might better have been open in saying " let

us defend the license of all who take upon themselves the marriage vow with a mental reservation, and the intent at some convenient time to disregard the solemn simplicity of its imperative command."

But let us return to the physician. Heretofore his misguided sense of the fitness of things has obscured his moral vision and blunted the sting of his conscience to such a degree that his tongue has failed to perform its duty, and even to-day would appear too palsied to tell its tale bravely and well. If a thorough reckoning could be had of the physical suffering and distress in this country, and of the lives blighted, and of the homes broken, all of which might have been saved had American medical men done their simple duty in telling the world all they knew, you would say to me that physicians had hardly earned the right to confer with the minister of the Gospel as to the enforcement of the Divine Commandment. The Puritan Fathers landed with a clean bill of moral health, beside which our own makes a discreditable showing. These facts are regretfully acknowledged by thousands of physicians, who to-day are endeavoring with feverish haste to undo the wrong which their timidity and false sense of propriety have perpetrated. Are they, however, alone in this fault of omission? Our sense of shame is hardly the less when we remember that the clergy have also encouraged the people to sell their birthright of virtue, together with the sanctity of home ideals, by themselves permitting and performing the rite of remarriage of libertines separated by the morally irresponsible law. If it be known in advance that no clergyman could be found on God's earth who would sanction the divorce by assisting the man or woman who had once violated the marriage vow to mock the Supreme Judge by a reassumption of the same vow with another husband or wife, at least one form of the leprosy of the twentieth century must die of inanition. It is idle to say, as some do, that the civil law would replace the clergyman. Civil authority has little weight with the dying man, and, generally speaking, would have just as little influence in the long run over the masses of the people who marry and are given in marriage. Man may scoff and trifle with the ordinary business of food-getting, and even jest aloud at the thought of a Supreme Deity; but in his heart he knows that there is a God, and consequently insists that the ceremonies of marriage and death are serious and divine affairs, not to be relegated to the magistrate and the mayor.

Thus the physician through failure to inform, and the clergyman, partly through ignorance of the scientific facts (his misfortune and again the physician's fault) resulting in a harmful use of the marriage ceremony, must bear together the yoke of responsibility for the social evil as it exists to-day. Theirs is the burden, and the load will continue pressing until their shoulders are applied in copartnership, and with a realization that they possess an ample, though slumbering power.

It is my purpose to lay before you the conditions as they exist in our country at the present moment, and subsequently to discuss the possibility and means of cure. With a view to presenting as compactly as possible a subject which, if exhaustively treated, would not find space in volumes or in days of time, I shall consider briefly three main features of the social evil:—

(1) Its prevalence in its various forms; (2) Its effect upon the individual and upon society at large; and (3) The attempts of the past to control and to eradicate this world-wide disease.

### PREVALENCE OF THE SOCIAL EVIL.

I shall retain the term, social evil, in order that what I have to say may be devoid of offense even to that portion of the public whose approval, at best half-willing, might be lost owing to sensibilities which prove stronger than conviction and conscience. Adultery, none the less, is the only term which completely characterizes the principle involved in the act of the libertine, married or single. Among the leisure classes it usually announces itself in the divorce courts, those market places and incubators of private immorality. It has recently been estimated that of every

9,900 marriages celebrated in this country about 500 (482) eventuate in divorce. You need not be told that the majority of these divorced individuals again marry, and not a few are divorced or separated a second time. With a considerable number the possibility of a divorce probably decides the rupture of a home circle, which might otherwise remain intact, and often become respectable, and perhaps affectionate and co-operative. During the last month there came to my notice a woman who had been unhappy in three matrimonial ventures, had been divorced from each of her helpmeets, remarried by clergymen, and who, when she attracted my attention, was marrying for the fourth time. It is not an infrequent occurrence for divorced men to marry divorced women without a scruple of conscience as to right or propriety. On the other hand, I must confess that I know of at least one instance in which the circumstances seemed to justify the strange confusion of fidelity to and disregard of the marriage vow. The exception, as usual, proves the rule. Just a week ago the newspapers published in black headlines the account of a prominent woman of one of our Eastern cities who obtained a divorce from her husband on the ground of desertion, and was remarried four hours later. In such an instance the object of the divorce was not separation, nor the right of woman to be free, but of prompt remarriage into an at least questionable state.

The onlooker is tempted to propound the Sadducee's question, " Whose wife of them is she? " Certainly not of the latter, rather than of the former husband, on the mere ground that the law has declared the marital obligation at an end. In the great majority of instances children have by their birth set a seal upon the first union. Of the 25,535 divorces granted in 1886, 65.8 per cent. were on petition of the wife, and in only 14.6 per cent. is the positive statement made that no children were born to the couple; while in 43 per cent. only is there no mention of the child in the legal proceedings, the presumption being that in more than the remaining 57 per cent. children had been born and had survived the divorce. An average of at least 2.07 children were born to each couple. What, I ask, must be the name of the act which confirms the second marriage of such a mother or father while the child's other parent still lives? Even the children notice and ponder over these happenings, and gain from them their first coating of moral callous, leading in a straight line to the conclusion that sexual purity is a commodity of doubtful existence and still more doubtful value.

As a proof that children observe and later contribute to the record of social evil, bears witness the flippant way in which those who have lately discarded the breast and bottle talk of "father and mother being separated," or "divorced," before they fully understand the meaning of the term. Such children marry, often before they have entered upon full womanhood or manhood, with an inborn light regard for the solemnity of the marriage rite that ensures an early swelling of the divorce records in the City Hall.

During the entire period 1877 to 1886 there were in the United States 444 divorces for every

10,000 marriages, as against 152 in Germany, 127 in France, and 19 in England. Thus there were in the United States alone during 1867 to 1886 8,330,000 marriages and 328,716 divorces granted, as against 258,332 in all of Europe. Of these 328,716 divorces, 67,686, or over 20 per cent., were obtained on the ground of adultery. The census of 1890 records 120,496 divorced persons in the United States. I have already quoted statistics to the effect that the divorce ratio has now risen to 482 per 9,900 marriages. Of the divorced individuals only the great minority fail to join themselves to and cohabit with other individuals, their former consorts making a no less indecent haste along the same highway.

It is but a step from the boudoir of the divorcee to the house of prostitution; too often just around the corner. To be sure, the chandeliers and the transom of the one are not brilliant with crimson coloring like those of the latter. There must be tasteful and refined obscurity in the immorality of educated people, whatever its nature. The fact is evident that the marriage vow is debauched and violated, though this furnishes no warrant for foregoing any of the regulations of wealth, position, aristocracy, and lineage. We will return at a later point to discuss this phase of the problem. For the moment let us proceed naturally in our study of the question.

There are at present in Philadelphia between 2,000 and 3,000 public prostitutes. New York City acknowledges between 40,000 and 50,000 abandoned women; and Chicago, although accurate figures are unobtainable, would appear to be afflicted with a larger army than either of the other cities. As a matter of fact, Chicago to-day, if we can draw an inference from the few figures at our command, supports as many prostitutes as Philadelphia and New York together. Even as far back as 1884 this central metropolis harbored, according to the police estimate, 302 houses of ill fame, with 1,097 regular inmates. During the World's Fair this number was doubled, if not trebled; and since that time Chicago has remained a vast cauldron of vice between the east and the center of the country. The prostitutes by their very existence, as well as openly on the street, invite boys and men from fourteen years upward to senility, and claim a large number as lasting patrons. Some few of these young and old male children learn an early lesson, and benefit by a severe experience. Many contract the habit-disease of sexual dissipation, of which they are never rid. I have found it necessary to come in contact with and see the inside of a considerable number of houses of ill fame, some decked with both human and inanimate furniture intended only for the rich, others of the meanest description. In one I found a young girl of twenty who told me her real name, and both the name and her sorry tale proved her to be the daughter of a cultivated home circle of which I know more than one member. Even so close to the fireside does the tempter creep.

In the center of the residence portion, and in the very block in which I lived until recently, stood a house built for and occupied by the mistress of one of the prominent politicians of your sister city. Every man, woman, and child within many squares knew there "was something wrong" with the woman who came and went through its doors. A near relative now occupies a house which was formerly altered and made attractive for still another Cleopatra by another municipal Mark Antony.

Fortunately the vice of a city is centered, as a rule, in a given locality, and as long as it is unmolested it keeps within its boundaries with considerable consistency. This is the state of affairs in your city and mine to such an extent that one may say a boy and girl must look for moral trouble in order to have it come their way. And yet we have seen that this is not invariably and strictly true. A gentleman of my acquaintance told me recently that he had found it necessary to take measures to prevent his son of sixteen years from indulging in sexual intercourse with a married woman who lived in the house opposite, and a friend of the family. His attention was called to the matter by the frequent visits of the boy to a home in which there were no juvenile attractions. The country boy, on the other hand, has at home few temptations and still fewer possibilities of mischief. Hence vice and resulting disease are much rarer in the rural districts than in the cities. The country boy needs, above all, safeguarding when in the city. Once let such innocent boys or girls have the length of the holiday rope, and unless their natural ignorance and curiosity are protected in advance or educated out of existence, in just the matters which you and I are discussing, they furnish the readiest and most easily yielding supply for the ever greedy demand of prostitution. One unfortunate phase of university and business life in a city is that it introduces these boys and young men, and too often young girls, to temptations and vicious conditions, and to unscrupulous companions, at a time when they are green as the grass on which they have been reared. Many go astray through ignorance, pure and simple. We have found this so true in my own University that we are taking the pains to warn the incoming class of each year with regard to the dangers of illicit sexual intercourse from the medical standpoint. The large universities are most seriously exposed. The smaller country colleges still retain at least the inestimable advantage of pure air for breathing purposes, and pure moral surroundings within which their students may expand mentally and manfully.

Even the preparatory school does not escape. Indeed, I question whether, in the light of that which I have seen, as well as from what I have learned since undertaking this study during the last few years, I would dare advise parents to send a young boy to one of the large boarding preparatory schools. One of my earliest patients, now a grown man, and intensely interested in the wish to prevent young boys from making his own mistake, has told me that he first entered a house of ill fame with a number of other boys when he was fifteen years of age, and a member of a junior class in a school nearer your city than it is to mine. He carried from the house, as did a number of his boy friends, a severe venereal infection. Other boys from the same school have recently told me that the practice has not died out, and that even younger boys are at times led into worse than mischief.

Another boy, now also a man, and formerly a member of one of our large Philadelphia schools, a short time ago told me much the same tale, giving me free permission to carry it to the head master providing I used no names. This I did about a year ago, and received the following reply:—

*My Dear Sir:—*

I have your letter of the 3rd inst. There is much that I might say in a personal interview which I cannot write. While I acknowledge, of course, the fact of the presence of that young man (who was formerly a student here) in your office, I have grave doubts in regard to the truth of the assertion he makes about others, because, being in a bad place himself, he is biased. To take such statements for what ought to be the results of careful investigation is to do wrong. . . . A long experience as head of a school has convinced me that the assertions of boys and young men as regards the institution which they attend may point the way to an investigation, but are unsafe to accept as results of such an investigation. . . . When I was at ——— College as a student the college numbered 60 men I was there four years. I knew every boy in the place and knew him well. There was but one on whom even a suspicion of such a thing could rest. . . . You seem to lose sight of the innocent, and there are plenty of them, I assure you. As a proof of it in my own case, I can say that no case has ever come within my knowledge. As a boy I was in ten different schools, boarding and day. That is, I have been associated with boys 50 years. I, of course, acknowledge the force of your *facts,* but I cannot from my own experience substantiate your inferences and the statements that have been made to you.

I remain etc., etc.

I laid his letter before his former pupil, who was equally astonished with me at the simplicity and unwillingness to listen of this friend and student of boys of 50 years' standing. His former charge said to me, " You may tell him that while I was in —— class at least ten of my classmates had had illicit intercourse with women, and some of us had gotten into trouble."

I wrote again, proposing to him to invite the parents of his boys to a brief meeting at which I should lay before them the details in my possession, asking them to decide whether the eyes of their boys should be opened regarding the certain consequences of their folly. I received the following ingenuous but evidently heartfelt reply:—

*My Dear Friend:—*

I have yours of the 1st inst. I thank you for writing me and also for sending me the pamphlet. I should not want for a moment to question the wisdom of approaching such a subject with college students, but I cannot feel that it would be right to enter upon it with my boys. Practically all my boys spend their time not at school in their own homes, under the care of parents who love them. I cannot see my way clear to get between them and their boys. In the matter of etc., etc. With great regard, I am

Yours faithfully,

The above, I regret to say, pictures fairly well the attitude of about one-quarter of the male public, one of mortified, injured unbelief. A full half of the remainder not only does not disapprove of what is going on of mischief in this old world, but often takes part in the proceeding. This portion of our people has prevented and is preventing moral progress by lowering the average tension of conscience and desire for betterment throughout the country at large. The remaining quarter represents the small circle of earnest fathers, physicians, and ministers of the Gospel who know the facts and are acting upon them. Possibly you ask the reason why boys cannot even now be thoroughly guarded against evil knowledge and against temptation.

Figures and statistics speak more plainly than argument. We have already noted the total of 80,000 to 100,000 prostitutes in the cities of New York, Philadelphia, and Chicago; Paris alone is estimated by her public officers to support 100,000; Berlin estimates her army at 40,000 to 50,000. We need say nothing whatsoever of the rest of the world, even of London with her 31,800 and upwards, to show the ease with which the young boy and man comes into contact with temptation. Of these prostitutes nearly one-half are not yet twenty years of age. Child-vice is anything but a myth. Probably no large city is free from the agents of the houses of prostitution, on the watch for the young girls who fill the rapidly decimating ranks of the army of sorrow. The Massachusetts Commission (Bureau of Statistics of Labor) has shown that the majority of these girls come directly from their homes. Contrary to the usual belief, comparatively few are actually married prior to prostitution. It was found that the following figures represented roughly the percentage of married women among those engaged in prostitution in the large cities.

New York ...........25. % (Sanger)
Boston ............... 7.65%
Chicago ..............25.6 %
Cincinnati ...........20.1 %
Louisville ...........26.6 %
New Orleans ......... 2.4 %
Philadelphia ......... 3.0 %
San Francisco .......25.08%

Of 3,866 prostitutes questioned, 1,236 (31.9%) had had no previous occupation, while 1,155 (29.8%) were engaged in housework, hotel service, table work, and cooking. Only 126 were saleswomen, and only 52 actresses, ballet girls, etc. Sanger reaches similar conclusions, and publishes like figures. Of this prostitute assembly from 40,000 to 50,000 die annually in the United

States, the average life being five or six years at their trade. No one year shows a marked decrease over the one preceding, the vacant ranks being at once filled by young and often previously innocent girls. The negro race furnishes no small number of the prostitutes in the large cities, many of these finding their patrons almost, if not quite, exclusively among white men. I well remember the remark of a fellow-student of my college days, now a physician, to the effect that he " found no pleasure in the society of a white woman." The observer needs merely to scan the constantly increasing army of mulattos and octoroons on our city thoroughfares to realize the extent to which the intercommunication of the races is progressing. There is also no doubt in my mind that this is one of the most fundamental explanations of the insubordinate and assertive effrontery of many of the northern negroes. The only doubt that remains in my mind is as to whether the term effrontery is justified under the circumstances.

Little wonder then that our boys learn early to

understand the pleasures and too often the consequences of sexual sin. Usually the sin is sought by the sinner, but in the face of these figures there should be no one with the temerity to say that evil is far to seek, and that an early warning is not required to save the average American boy. It will many a time require more than the pastor's example and personal plea, and the warning and affectionate assurance of the family physician that if a man honors his mind and body, both body and mind will honor him. It will need the intelligent instruction of both the mother and father, and the home influence; and God pity the boy who has neither. I shall have more to say of the thoroughness of the saturation of this country with the social evil when I meet you again. A word now regarding the

RESULTS OF THE SOCIAL EVIL IN 'AMERICA.

First, with reference to the individual. I would place the responsibility for the gradual disappearance of the American home circle, one of our prized institutions, equally at the door of those who are guilty of marital infidelity and at that of the average remarried divorcee and his half-sister and brother, the male and female prostitute. When we record 325,000 and upward of American homes disrupted during ten years in the divorce court, and 70,000 and odd of these openly laid at the threshold of adultery, we have said enough to stir the most slothful to activity, if only the public knew what is most vital to its permanence and character. What a wilfully slow and ignorant thing the public is! Three hundred thousand loyal new Christian homes scattered here and there throughout the land would exert an influence at once so masterful and far-reaching as to win it for clean living. Three hundred thousand divorces mean that the morals of the community are on a gallop down hill. And yet I believe that by raising their hands the physicians and clergymen of America can, in a great measure, stem this tide.

In home breaking you have heard my most serious charge, for with its passing goes also the American pride in the family name that serves as the last restraint against wrongdoing. There is still another form of home breaking of which few of you will hear until your work leads you among the common people, the factory and the laboring population. It is also the result of and a form of the social evil. One of your fellow-citizens pictures it in a letter from the Educational Alliance. "We are called upon every evening by deserted wives," and "a noticeable element common to most of these cases is that the women are about to become mothers." Many bigamy cases result, the woman living with the first man who offers immediate support, with or without the form of marriage. Do you wonder at her decision? What would you be likely to do in her place?

Only second in importance is the widespread series of venereal diseases, polymorphous, and transmitted not only by sexual intercourse, but, in the event that an innocent person is infected, with equal rapidity if not with equal frequency, by all the graces of affection, by the kiss, the embrace, from mother to son, from daughter to father, and the circle around. New York is estimated as to-day harboring 225,000 persons infected with syphilis, and about 800,000 suffering from gonorrhœa in the acute and chronic forms. Not one of these persons can fail to infect some other who continues the endless chain. Sturgis estimated that there are annually 50,000 new cases of syphilitic infection in New York City, each of which at once becomes a new focus for the spread of the disease. The greatest danger is to wives and mothers, and thence to all with whom they come in contact. Occasionally a physician will be heard venturing the assertion that his experience does not bear out these statements, and that the danger is greatly overdrawn. He is convinced only by the statistical record of cases observed in great cities like New York, Philadelphia, and Chicago.

I have as yet made no reference to the widespread distribution of venereal diseases among the prostitute class. It is sufficient to say that no prostitute can ply her or his trade long without suffering venereal infection, and that most, if not all, carry these diseases in a chronic form, which renders them practically incurable, and permanently a source of danger to those with whom they associate. Nearly a half of several thousand questioned openly acknowledged infection. Statistics show that as a result of cohabitation with these women over 50 per cent. of all young men in this country are infected with some form of venereal disease before their thirtieth year. Nor do American wives fail to suffer as the result of this harvest. Morrow states that there is more venereal infection among virtuous wives than among professional prostitutes in this country; a statement which, while extreme, at least shows the serious attitude of mind with which the condition of affairs is regarded by those who make it their special study. He also submits the following figures: Allow that 8 per cent. of the 16,000,000 married women in this country are infected by gonorrhœa (instead of the 80 per cent. estimated by Noeggerath in writing of venereal disease among the wives of New York City); this, he says, " would give over one and a quarter million (women) infected from gonorrhœa alone " in the United States of America. This estimate is at least within the limits of probability, and is undoubtedly far too low.

The report of the Committee of Seven of New York City showed that 30 per cent. of all instances of venereal infection seen in private practice among women are due to the husband's gonorrhœa; while Fournier proved that 25 per cent. of all syphilitic women seen in private practice were similar so-called "innocent" infections, and that of the married women infected with syphilis 75 per cent. of all cases originated with the husband. Every instance of such infection, of course, represents one or more examples of previous illicit intercourse, or, more politely speaking, the social evil.

The ultimate result is octopus-like in its influence. Statistics show that 50 per cent. of all married women infected with gonorrhœa, namely, 50 per cent. of at least 1,250,000 women in this country (calculating still from the almost ridiculously small 8 per cent.) are sterile. If some one would inform President Roosevelt of this fact, he would perhaps allow American mothers a breathing interval before reassuring them as to the horror of wilful sterility, when physically capable of bearing children. Neither the President, nor the wife, and ofttimes not even the family physician, suspects the presence of a latent infection. Too often the physician knows it certainly and protects the husband by a judicious but manifestly unfair silence. It is high time the President turned his strenuous gaze in intelligent pity upon those mothers who cannot beget children because of the 50 per cent. of our young men who contract venereal disease before they have arrived at a marriageable age. However great the justification for his observation when first made, there must have been many such among the audiences which he has chided for their supposed selfish desire for a small and select family circle.

In France, where such statistics are recorded, we find that 20-25,000 children die annually of hereditary syphilis. A far greater number never live to die. In America, where venereal diseases are not even discussed by the laity for false modesty's sake, it would seem at least advisable to give heed to the fact that 25 per cent. of all the blindness in the world is being caused by one venereal disease, gonorrhœa, and many more cases by its congener, syphilis. We not only make no public record of these matters, but our journals refuse to publish the facts, because they are too bald.

And finally, for I have already given you more than enough food for reflection during the short period before we continue this discussion, just a word regarding the

## ATTEMPTS OF THE PAST TO CONTROL AND ERADI-CATE THE SOCIAL EVIL.

In Europe, as well as in America, nearly every known method has been made the object of experiment, from moral suasion down to deliberate licensing of the prostitute class, individually and collectively, in houses of legalized ill repute. In Vienna I have seen the cards issued to these women, licensing them to ply their trade, and supposedly guaranteeing them at the time of issuing the card to be free from venereal disease.

In France and Germany hundreds are examined at intervals by officially appointed physicians, who, as far as it is possible, scrutinize these unfortunate beings in the hope of preventing a portion of the harm they may do to humanity in response to humanity's own lustful invitation. St. Louis, in our own country, has tried the same measure. The general verdict may be epitomized in the comment of Lecour, the Prefect of Paris, who finds that " prostitution is increasing in Paris in spite of the strictest regulation." In nearly all the European countries the regulation laws are being or have been repealed as not only worthless but disadvantageous to the cause. Registration died a stormy death in St. Louis four years after it was adopted.

In certain cities the world over, and in this country, the first notable example abroad being Rome, the attempt was instituted to confine the prostitute class within one section or locality. This has also invariably failed. It has so far partially succeeded only in those instances in which the isolation and localization has been spontaneous; never when enforced by law, because such enforcement is beyond human power.

Rarely, and I am glad to say only rarely in recent years, has the effort been systematically made to punish the female unfortunate; for in the long run she is an unfortunate, and often abhors her mode of living and the sin of it all. She suffers as certainly as she injures, and in a few short years meets her inevitable doom, death from disease. She is then with her Maker, who knows her better and has more pity for her than you or I. The skirts of **A**lmighty Justice are spotlessly clean, and cover a benevolence that is incomprehensible to those who are most severe in their professed integrity and have yet allowed themselves to carry on or condone this abomination since the world began.

The attempts of the past, we may conclude, have one and all proved signal failures. This the figures and facts which I have cited conclusively show. The outlook from many standpoints is indeed a dark one from the very nature of things. The right of suffrage rests within the hand of the male member of society. Up to date he has failed to provide for the correction of the male sinner, and is likely to if the solution of the problem be left altogether to him. It must also be noted that as usual that portion of the world which is working at all, is starting from the wrong end of things and is attempting to cure a canker the nature and cause of which it does not yet understand. It does not yet realize that strict virtue has not attained par value. You will also find physicians, and even so-called specialists in venereal disease, who will admit the accuracy of all the figures I have laid before you, and yet ridicule the possibility and advisability of an attempt at betterment or cure. A certain few in their crass ignorance even deny the facts. These few, moreover, are virulent, and have rendered difficult the most hopeful of all the methods in our reach, the only one that has not had a thorough trying out, viz.: the education of our women and children in the laws of physiology, of health, and of their free-born physical and moral rights, and the right to demand them. As a matter of fact we must confess that we are only beginning to succeed in a battle centuries old.

What will you and I conclude in this serious matter? Is the social evil incurable at the present time? I think we must answer " yes, under existing circumstances, and as long as it enjoys the sleek, contented, participating inactivity of the people!" Is there any prospect of its disappearance in our children's time? Probably not, owing largely to the indifference or positively bad influence of many fathers and mothers, and of much of the literature of the day. Another most potent influence in rendering the existence of the prostitute possible, and often profitable, is the certainty that there will be sufficient patronage for them all for at least a sufficient period for the extinction of our present youngest generation. Many of the latter have inherited from their parents an almost uncontrollable lustful desire. There is a likelihood, however, that your children and mine can be individually protected and educated in the knowledge of good and evil, if you and I personally see to it, and that the social crime can be lim-

ited to the lowest and to the openly libertine portion of the so-called higher classes.

Is there indeed ground for the hope that our
children's children will see the day in which marriage shall have become an altogether sacred institution, a day in which adultery shall be unhesi-
tatingly called by the name stamped upon it by
the Supreme Judge, and a day in which men and
women as well as boys and girls shall set a watch
upon their towers to guard and keep them pure
against the final reckoning?

To this question I answer affirmatively without
reserve. Vice is indeed a disease-habit, not a
mere custom grown into, and easily, or even with
difficulty, discarded. It can be uprooted trunk
and branch years hence if the starvation process
be begun now. Only that which is nourished can
live. In its worst light we must look upon immorality as a human sore, involving moral fibres
which have long been on the verge of malignancy;
but which can yet be stimulated into healthy
growth. In its best illumination it may be seen
in the far distance as a plague, conquered by in-

telligent prevention begun to-day and continued forever. Prevention implies the ethical training of American mothers and fathers, and, through them, of the present and of the coming American infancy. The Hand that wrote upon the tables of stone "Thou Shalt Not Commit Adultery" is able and inevitably must enforce the command. Only the thoughtless and the hopeless dare conclude that immorality can find justification and permanence in the eternal plan. Somewhere and somewhen you and I will be held strictly accountable not only for all the wrong we have done, but for all we have failed to prevent, our accountability being measured by the breadth of our vision, and by the talent in our keeping. I cannot conceive of an All-wise Justice that will sanction or condone a compromise with this evil, or a lack of hopefulness as to the final result. Time flies swiftly. What is impossible to-day will be inexplicably easy to-morrow. Your influence and mine have their value in God's sight, if not in that of our fellows. Morality and pure living have few champions whose loyalty can stand the final test.

The church itself is full of slothfulness, insincerity, and covered sin. The public standard of morals, when all the returns are in, is low. Your standard and mine have been too low; otherwise we would not have come together tonight. The demand for the disappearance of this scourge has neither become active nor general, and will not until there is a deeper intelligence and awakening. But from behind all the discouragement of the task, and beneath and throughout all the weariness of the struggle that is before you and me, if we engage in the battle for the preservation of the home circle and a clean America, beams forth with a brilliancy and a certainty that are as constantly and newly refreshing as the promise is old, the legend

" He that keepeth Israel shall neither slumber nor sleep! "

You and I are not working alone. I never hear a man or woman venture the assertion that the social evil is a necessary institution, and impossible of remedy (and I have heard clergymen, even, make this claim), without hearing, as it were, in the distance the prophet calling, "Is the Lord's Hand waxed short?" "Shall the clay say to him that fashioneth it, What makest thou? or thy work, He hath no hands?"

"God needs best men to help Him," but in the finality of things, if the efforts of best men fail, there are still the Everlasting Arms which will gather the harvest of good and bad, and enfold all that is worthy of nobility and of the crown of life. The embrace will repay every effort and every energy spent in keeping one child or ten thousand thousand children pure and true.

# IV

## THE RELATION OF THE CITIZEN TO THE SOCIAL EVIL.*

"'WHAT is Truth?' said jesting Pilate; and would not stay for an answer." When Bacon quoted these words, he must have been looking forward in his mind's eye to some such condition of affairs as exists in the America of the twentieth century, and to her indifference to the social evil in her midst. Again by this term let me include not only the avocation of the scarlet woman, but just as certainly the lust and looseness of morals, home and public, that dot here and there almost every walk in life.

The answer to Pilate's jest rings painfully clear

* Address to the students of Union Theological Seminary, April 14, 1905.

117

in the ears of the American citizen, and yet he waves it by. The public is in fact a gigantic Pontius Pilate, asking with the same semi-seriousness, " What is truth? " and closing both ears and eyes, and turning its back to the answer. It has not wanted social purity or it would have had it long since.

Bacon also said that " Clear and round dealing is the honor of man's nature, and that mixture of falsehood is like alloy in coin of gold and silver, which may make the metal work the better, but it embaseth it." America has traduced her own nature in postponing clear and round dealing in this matter of public morals and in closing her ears to the cry that is going up within and around her borders. That I have exaggerated in no particular the extent to which her robes have been soiled, you will admit upon the simple basis of the facts laid before you at our previous meeting. That we can still square our moral account is, however, equally true, and I wish with this as our object, to discuss our position as individual citizens with relation to both legalized and criminal sexual immorality.

A vital question must again be propounded and answered at the outset: Is the social evil in any respect a necessary institution? Of course the only possible advantage would be that of physical need. From the physical standpoint, however, it certainly is not necessary. There is at the present time no reason for doubt as to the attitude of the medical profession upon this point. If there is any principle that has been thoroughly established by the consensus of medical opinion it is that neither man nor woman has been fashioned in such a way by the Creator as to render it impossible or even deleterious to the general welfare to remain continent, in the strictest natural meaning of the word, throughout an entire life. The married state undoubtedly realizes the highest and most complete fulfilment of physical and moral happiness, and yet in the face of centuries of contrary teaching the twentieth century physician must in all honesty tell you that no man nor woman has ever been physically or morally benefited by illicit indulgence. Thousands who have permitted themselves to enter upon the practice — which, when once begun, medical history tells you, is at once a habit-disease — have ruined physical health and mentality, and at the same time brought disease and suffering upon those around them.

With the boy, the natural question is, Is it right? Is it worth while? Do I dare to run the risk for curiosity's sake, or to escape ridicule? With the grown man the desire for novelty has degenerated into a search for sexual pleasure, and the wrong done to his true self and to the partner of his excesses fades dimly away behind the too often deliberate misapprehension that he is responding to one of Nature's imperative demands. One of your fellow-townsmen, to whom I referred at the time of my previous meeting with you, intimates in his closing paragraph that enforced chastity will result in disease, which, he says, " is the usual vengeance of outraged nature." Either ignorance or a wicked carelessness of the truth inspires every such statement. I feel that the young man who reads it, and decides for the sale of his and another's soul as against a virtuous life, may with some semblance of justice twine a wreath of reproaches around the author's brow, and lay heavily upon him the responsibility for a new wave of wrongdoing in this land of ours, into which every year pours enough of the old world's dregs to satisfy our worst cravings.

The morally loose woman acts upon much the same motive. The only distinction that I would draw between the mental attitude of the two sexes in respect to sexual sin is that in the woman it is, with probably a few exceptions, the expression of a deliberate badness, with " the devil may care " as the inscription upon her insignia; while with the man the fault usually follows and is screened by the attempted excuse of physical necessity, believed in not a whit, but undoubtedly exerting a soporific effect upon the conscience and power of self-control. Neither sex honestly and within the inmost soul has ever thought that the transgression was right or justifiable in the sight of the Supreme Judge. In the eyes of the people this has always been and will be "the unpardonable sin" just so long as it applies to someone other than oneself. Unpardonable it is indeed when weighed in the balance of our own frail virtues and consciences, but thank God there is still reason for both man and woman to rise with faces turned upward toward better things, even if the fall has been as low as man's limit of forgiveness.

We gravitate then inevitably to the query, Is the social evil either necessary or expedient from the standpoint of public polity? Would society at large be better or worse in the home and on the highway if all forms of illicit sexual indulgence could be done away with? Certainly not expedient, if we base our decision upon the direct results upon society. In your city and mine there seems to be little or no reason for doubt that many members of the police force have been rendered morally and financially corrupt as the result (1) of the determination on the part of loose women to ply their trade; (2) of the constant, though none too strong pressure of public opinion which renders the business of the prostitute intermittently precarious 'for appearance' sake'; and (3) of the deliberate shielding (for the sake of money return) of wrongdoers by those who ought to conserve, not destroy, the public morals. In certain cities not only have houses of prostitution been freely used as centers of false registration of voters, usually fictitious, so that city rulers have been chosen and elected outright with the aid of just such a libidinous majority, but the houses of policemen have sometimes served this purpose. There seems also to be no doubt that at certain elections in Philadelphia thousands of illegal votes were cast, of which no small number were registered from these allied dwellings of the open enemies and of the guardians of the law.

One more step, now limiting the influence of the social evil to the home circle and to the individual. Shroeder has claimed that chastity tends toward disease. When I read his statement I wondered how he arrived at his conclusion, and whether it could possibly be an honest one. The medical authority upon whose dictum he bases his assertion, who himself had left wife and home to enjoy the embraces of a paramour, even he never dared to claim that illicit sexual intercourse either prevented disease or debility in any form, or the converse, that the practice had ever proved anything but deleterious to the physical health of mankind. How does Shroeder's statement of pathology due to virtuous living measure alongside that which finds its immediate origin in sexual sin? According to the census of 1900 there were voluntarily reported during the census year 1,591 deaths in the United States from venereal disease, 934 males and 657 females, a proportion compared with the mortality from all causes of 1.6 per 1,000. This total (1,591 deaths) represents only a fraction of the entire number if we include the unreported mortality from direct sequelae of venereal disease, such as the inevitable changes in the blood vessels, the heart, and the kidneys, apoplexy, locomotor ataxia, and kindred diseases of the nervous system.

Not even the average physician realizes how frequent and wide-spread the instances of extragenital, usually innocent, infection have come to be. Among 9,058 cases gathered from medical literature* of extragenital syphilis alone, 1,810 cases presented the initial sore upon the lip, 1,148 upon the breast, 734 inside the mouth, 432 on the finger and hand, 372 about the eye, 307 on the tonsil, and many elsewhere on the surface of the body. The foregoing are, of course, only a small number compared with those which remain unrecognized, undiscovered, or unreported by the observer. The highest death rate among the reported cases occurred among the children under 15 years of age. Some of these were instances of innocent infection, many of hereditary syphilis, and a certain number resulted from deliberate sexual intercourse between children, usually of the tenement house classes. There are many instances on record of child vice, small armies of little boys being infected by a tiny girl, who when detected in her mischief has boasted of the number of conquests she had made. In more than a few instances a small boy has been a similar offender. This cradle immorality brings us very close to the center

* Bulkeley, 1905.

of the American home, and we glance instinctively at the table upon which the large Bible once had its place. Is it still there, or has the novel claimed a better right to recognition? And is the novel clean, or does it help on the cause of unrestrained immorality?

In 1880 there were 1,577,000 births in the United States, of which fifty-five out of every one thousand were illegitimate. During 1900 there were 2,049,132 births recorded in this country, representing of course only an incomplete total and a mere working basis for computation. Of these it is estimated that about 70 in every 1,000 were illegitimate offspring. In England at the same time it was estimated that of every 1,000 births 54 were illegitimate; in France, 74; in Germany, 87; and in Austria, 135.

Bertillon's statistics show that on an average 100 prostitutes will give birth to about 60 children during their lifetime, thus accounting for the comparatively small number of illegitimates as compared with the total number born. To be sure the total is large enough to be a warning of some value to both men and women who are intelligent enough to weigh the consequences of illegitimate paternity and maternity. Within sight of my summer home is a large building devoted to the care of foundling children, the harvest of the social evil, and of marital infidelity.

But there is another phase of the problem which must appeal to every thinking man and woman. There were in the United States in 1900 7,833,492 boys between 10 and 20 years of age, and 6,948,-123 young men between 20 and 30 years. On these 14,000,000 boys and young men you will naturally concede must rest at some future time not only the political future of the nation, but its physical and moral health, and its freedom from or contamination with venereal disease. I have previously mentioned to you the fact based on careful statistics that over 50 per cent. of all young men in this country are infected with some form of venereal disease before they reach the age of 30. Thus 50 per cent. of nearly seven million (6,948,123) young men were undoubtedly, either at that time victims of venereal disease, or were supposedly and sometimes actually cured of previous venereal infection. Of the remaining eight million (7,833,492) between 10 and 20 years, over 50 per cent. have now been or will have been infected before the year 1920 arrives. From 15 to 20 per cent. of the entire number of these males are infected before their twenty-first year; 50 to 60 per cent. before their twenty-fifth year; and about 75 per cent. before their thirtieth year.

As against these figures there were in this country 7,802,831 females between 10 and 20 years, and 6,916,334 between 20 and 30, alive in 1900. Of these very many were and are doomed to infection by the 7,000,000 and odd young men whom medical experience marks as certain to carry venereal disease. These figures also point directly at the heart of the difficulty. The boy, I thoroughly believe, should be the object of your main attack, or shall I say of your most persevering, fearless, affectionate education. If you err at all it will be in telling him too little. If you tell him more than he need know you will be surprised at the manliness with which he will handle his individual problem, unless you have armed him too late. The difficulty is to determine when to open his eyes. I believe your duty as clergymen and ours as medical men is to awaken the fathers and mothers, and to urge them, especially the former, to a realization of their duty in preventing evil to their children. Compared with the mother the average father is a moral coward. The work is rightfully his, yet the mother must do it, and as usual does it better than he. I know of more than one mother who has gathered her boys around her, some almost full grown, and read to them the plain figures and facts with reference to illicit intercourse and venereal disease which were presented to the students of my University in 1903. If you will attend to this phase of the contest the parents will themselves win for you the boy and the girl, the future man and woman. If the parents send them to you, you now have the knowledge that will help you in the most difficult of all tasks, that of preparing a pure boy or girl for contact with the evil in the world in such a manner that no harm will ensue. It can be done, and is being done every day by a few earnest fathers and mothers; and if it is not done eventually throughout the length and breadth of the land the responsibility will justly fall upon you and me. Here lies your work and mine, and a mountain-load it appears at the start. If you can preach these figures loudly and clearly enough you will make deaf America hear. Once let the public realize the full significance of such statistics and red heat will become white, and no official who is willing to wink at a single instance of individual or municipal sin will find a square inch cool enough to rest upon, or a municipality which will tolerate even a hurried and uncomfortable sitting.

Crittenton estimated some years ago that there were at the minimum 300,000 prostitutes in the continental United States alone, of whom 50,000 died annually, their places being filled by accessions from abroad and from the formerly innocent classes at home. Mr. Richard Wells estimates that Philadelphia harbors 2,000 of these unfortunate beings, a figure which I believe to be considerably below the actual number, even if we limit our count to those who ply their trade as public vendors of immorality. My work among the students of a large university has brought to my attention also a considerable number of supposedly and apparently respectable young women and girls, who for pleasure's sake and regardless of the risk, indulge in sexual intercourse with equally respectable young men, without thought of financial gain. Occasionally this occurs as the result of a promise of subsequent marriage; but far more frequently in the instances that have come to my personal notice the motive has been impatience at sexual restraint, and an impulsive, heedless act which, when once safely undertaken, has paved the way to a practice which always ends in catastrophe. The women in these instances reach the physician in one of two conditions, pregnancy or venereal disease, and nearly always the latter is experienced with or without the former. The clergyman learns of the case in one of two ways; either through some kindly sheltering influence, such as the Woman's Directory in my own city, or in some instances through an open confidence in her pastor by an erring girl who knows not which way to turn in her distress. Many also are the so-called shop girls, who receive from three to five dollars per week, from which they must clothe and support themselves, and often contribute to the home fund. A little unusual pressure upon such a girl, with the certainty that for a brief time at least she can earn from two to ten times the amount of her weekly wage by a life which under different circumstances she would abhor, and she may yield to seeming or real necessity, as it appears to her at the time. Once she has given away or sold her honor, the great motive for restraint, an unsullied virtue, is gone. These girls are not public prostitutes; some few of them, indeed, never accept a penny of ill-gotten gain. But when they do under circumstances of true need, I have more real sympathy for them than for the diamond-bedecked lady who discards one husband in the morning and is the bride of another before night.

Another of the most serious consequences with

which you and I will have to deal is that of illegitimate father- and motherhood. From the standpoint of all three — father, mother, and child — the world looks down for a moment with a frown; from the sorry faces of the latter two its curse is never allowed to pass away. Unfortunately for him and for the people at large, the man, sooner or later, resumes his place in society, and his error is lost sight of as time flies.

In 1880 there were 1,577,000 births in this country, of which 86,735 were illegitimate, or 55 per 1,000 births. In 1896 in England and Germany the proportion was respectively 42 and 91 per 1,000 births. I have already quoted the statistics in the United States for 1890, in which it appears that 70 of every 1,000 births, or 143,430 in all, were illegitimate. Many of these births resulted from the first lapse from moral integrity on the part of the woman. Probably in no instance in which a young woman has been willingly tempted or unwillingly violated has the man been a new offender. And yet the woman suffers the punishment and the man goes scot free!

No figures can compute the mental anguish endured before these girls give up the fight for virtue, and before they acknowledge themselves members of the army of prostitution. Can you imagine yourself more helpless as a physician or a pastor than when a refined woman, or even a simple uneducated servant girl comes to you with the news that she is to mother a child, and that the father has either left her to her fate, or is morally too low to be held responsible? The public suggests, " Make him marry the woman and support the child." The woman replies, " Where is he, that I may marry him? " or, just as frequently, cannot bear to look on his face. The physician is called upon to destroy the child, and Christian fathers and mothers beg that it may be done to save a daughter in distress. He declines to commit murder and at once loses his influence with all three, who eventually find some one to commit the crime at the risk of his fair name, and, as you and I believe, of his soul.

I have merely sketched for you one such case. Very often the termination of it all is the departure from home of the girl, and an entrance into a brief immoral life, the unhappiness of which has nowhere been pictured so graphically as in Samuel Johnson's portrayal of Misella, the prostitute. I saw in my office not long since the daughter of a Presbyterian elder, pregnant by a young man, both members of the church, and the man a former Sunday School teacher. Both desired, even demanded, a criminal operation to save her reputation and his; and when I refused they went elsewhere to find some charlatan who would comply with what they believed, under the circumstances, to be the only procedure worthy of their consideration. There is only one way in which such a girl can be reclaimed. If her parents or some outside motherly influence will bravely and loyally shield her during this time, so that the chill blast of public opinion may be altogether avoided or ignored by those who love the sorry, bent figure of the unwilling mother, she may be won into a love for her child and into a life of which she may still be not ashamed. Under any other circumstances the girl is doomed.

For every one that is saved dozens slip away along the easy incline as soon as need or inclination urges in this direction. Only the other day I heard a noble woman say that, after many years of work among fallen women, she did not feel sure that she had done much real and permanent good, so regularly had they returned to the ways from which they had been supposedly reclaimed. Still another worker has found that not 3 per cent. of the prostitutes are permanently reclaimed. On the other hand, Dr. Abbey and her co-workers have lost but 3 per cent. of all the young women (not prostitutes) who have been reached during their first illegitimate pregnancy. This is one of the most fruitful phases of the prevention which John Locke claimed was "better than cure, and far cheaper." I have myself talked with a number of acknowledged prostitutes from the simple viewpoint of their physical condition and have invariably received the reply, "What can I do? Go back to three dollars a week?"

This need of, and this ready method of, money-getting is not only the problem we must at once face, but it is one of the most active causes of the trouble, and an influence which lies constantly in wait for the young man and woman of to-day, especially when Providence has permitted the woman to be nurtured in the lap of a municipality.

A word now regarding the male offender. You will find him in every walk of life, in the shop, in the factory, in the teacher's chair, in the Sabbath School, and occasionally in the pulpit, as the newspapers have forced us to observe. The man with the most open countenance, as well as he with a sinister expression; the senile subject, who may, like Thomas Parr, be sued for adultery at 118 years of age, or the boy of six or seven; all have like passions and many indulge them, ofttimes to their own disadvantage and discomfiture. Still more often results the sorrow of their companion in crime. I have gradually become convinced that the tendency in the boy and girl is at first in the direction of purity of thought and action. Sooner or later some bird of evil omen in the guise of an unprincipled nurse or an unscrupulous companion plants the seed that results in sorrow and suffering. I have already stated my belief that boarding schools in many cases exert a vicious influence over both boys and girls at a most impressionable time. I have heard more young men ascribe their first departure from virtuous living to boarding school influences than to any other single cause. Current literature and the stage alike encourage a flippancy in dealing with vice, and a callous, indifferent attitude toward its presence and prevalence. One seldom reads a popular novel without meeting very early in the story with one or more instances of moral obliquity. The most popular play circles round some broken home, and twines as intimately with infidelity and divorce as the vine and the tree. The social evil is already so well established in our midst that we smile at the man or woman as warmly and intimately after the moral lapse as before. We buy tickets in order to give our children the opportunity to hear at a tender age the innate nastiness and immorality of an artificial and overdone society upon the stage. The conversation of men and women of our day is such as to cause wonder with regard to the type of offspring to be expected from such fathers and mothers.

And yet this old world, I doubt not, is better than it has ever been. It is to me a brave sign that we are noting these things. I think we are wrong in believing them new. Conditions are probably far more favorable to their rank growth than heretofore, and at this moment the weeds are simply pushing their heads above the wall. Such occurrences must become offensive before you and I begin to take our reckoning. We must realize that in your city, as in mine, men, women, and children are crowded together in a sinful-manner that engenders crime, and renders it rather the natural than an abnormal thing. Kennaday, in writing of the "one hundred lodging houses" of New York City, states that they are licensed to contain 16,470 beds; and, adding the small hotels, over 20,000 beds. He mentions one house in Greenwich street in which three families with seven children make their home, the only entrance to which is "through a dirty saloon, mostly occupied by farmers and truck-gardeners, all grown men." We can hardly expect a child to grow clean and pure of mind and body in the midst of tobacco smoke, alcohol, foul language, and an immoral and obscene humanity. And yet even this class is not a hopeless one. I have said before, and I repeat here, that, if the physician and clergyman clasp hands and act with intelligent and affectionate sympathy for a portion of humanity which has fallen exceedingly low in the moral scale, both the young man and the young woman can be finally won. The mother and the father are the only possible medium, and childhood almost the only available time.

One other class of influences I would mention before discussing the ways and means of controlling this widespread disease: There seems to be no doubt that tobacco and alcohol are two factors creating and lending strong encouragement to immoral tendencies in both man- and womankind. Probably no one will ever know how many men have found the way to illicit intercourse made possible by alcoholic intoxication, meaning by this not drunkenness, but the ordinary effect of alcohol upon the moral as well as the physical sense. To a lesser degree the same assertion can be made regarding tobacco. Probably there are not ten habitues of the houses of prostitution in this land who do not smoke or drink, or both. I have heard more than one young man state that as long as he avoided these two drugs he had no difficulty in controlling other passions. Even though I myself was reared in a cloud of tobacco smoke, I must say with all candor that the clergyman and the physician appear to me to have less right than any other human being to injure and depress the powers loaned to them by the Almighty by the use of stimulants and narcotics in even the smallest quantities. If these drugs cause harm to others, and if influence is an indispensable feature of our daily lives, as we know it to be, then you and I cannot explain away our responsibility if we openly or secretly submit ourselves to these allies of immorality. I again speak strictly as a physician, not as an enthusiast in the crusade against tobacco and alcohol as such.

## WHAT PRACTICAL METHODS CAN BE USED AGAINST THE SOCIAL EVIL?

History says none! Are there indeed no available methods? History has been mistaken prior to this, and in spite of her negative, history's echo rings out "Yes!"

The past has failed and failed ingloriously. Europe has tried every method that has been suggested. Registration, licensing, segregation, have failed in France, Austria, and Germany. All of these countries, like America, are overrun with prostitution and venereal disease. In France 75 per cent. of the adult males are supposed to have syphilis. In the United States, many of these measures have been instituted, and we still support upward of 300,-000 prostitutes and a corresponding prevalence of venereal disease. In spite of this record of ignominious failure the suggestion has been made that these same measures be established in Philadelphia in the near future. A few weeks ago, when my city began to agitate against its crime centre, a body of ladies in Washington wrote an indignant letter protesting against the new influx of prostitutes in their municipality, just as they had accomplished a reform. Thus hemmed in by former failure and by the ignorance and apathy of the public, also by the participation in the evil by that very public, the contest must be fought uphill, and with the covert, sometimes the open, opposition of every class of society. Do you ask what the echo means, and how success can be accomplished? I answer, How do you cure a child of any bad habit? By telling him not to repeat it? Certainly not, if you wish to have your lesson learned. You explain what that habit will lead to; a burn if the fire is played with, a fall if the stairs are not avoided; and you repeat and persist in the education of the mind to associate cause and result. The public is composed of grown children, who will never lose their childish way of thinking; indeed all they lose is the child's honesty of purpose and their own former openness and honesty of method in sinning. Amongst other object lessons you have somewhat over 50,-

000 totally blind persons to point your argument, from 10 to 20 per cent. of whom were doomed to darkness owing to venereal disease, usually of the male parent. In one recent year 136 new cases of gonorrhœal ophthalmia were reported in the city of New York. There are also the thousands of unhappy homes, the hundreds of otherwise unnecessary surgical operations upon your mothers and sisters, and the dead children who might have lived, and the changelings born who might better have died. These facts will form subject matter enough when you approach the parent. Now begin on the child through the latter, and let him understand, and let the young girl understand, all that their ages will warrant, of the meaning and purpose of the sexual portion of their make-up. Gather the young men together once a year at least and let some physician whom they respect inform them of the dangers of trifling with a God-given talent. Teach each young woman to demand in her husband the same clean, open record that she lays before him, and let her know how comparatively few of the men of to-day

can bring to her an unsullied honor. Tell her that she holds the key to the problem, and that if she wishes the men of her acquaintance to be morally and physically clean, to insist that they shall be pure individually, and in their particular relation to her; not that ' mankind ' shall be pure, a favorite demand of the woman's club, and one forgotten when the proposal of marriage is made. Wyoming has given woman the full right of suffrage for thirty years, and has recorded more marriages and fewer divorces than any other State in the Union. This fact implies that there is at once less adultery where the woman is in charge with her eyes open and with authority to command. Let her know that to marry a man of loose, especially of drinking, habits, means for herself the likelihood of venereal disease, perhaps an operation, and not infrequently, death; that it often results in a miscarriage or the birth of a dead child, or still worse, in the delivery of one that can never be healthy; and that her unhappiness is the certain reminder of her husband's sin and her own blind folly. Tell her also that 50 per cent. of the young men of this country are infected before they marry, and you not only arm her against infection, but you prevent the disease in the future man. The woman will not retire until she has won her fight, because she alone is honest in the presentation of the subject, having nothing to hide and no conscience to soothe. Only the man is playing the role of the hypocrite, and only the wife has a record that will enable her to apprehend him in it. It will not require more than a few generations before men will learn that they must offer themselves to their prospective wives as clean, morally and physically, as the women come to them. There is no law of justice or equity that provides for male indulgence and for female chastity. There need be no appeal to the courts to provide for a certificate of health on the part of the man and woman who contract in marriage. Tell the woman in advance how often the abdomen is opened as the result of a husband's former indiscretion, and she will marry only that man who is above suspicion in all his habits and tendencies, and who neither fears nor hesitates to prove the fact. You then have your battle half won. The physician can strengthen your attack by corroborating every statement you have made. He can and soon will co-operate with his patient in demanding as a matter of easily established right and custom the proof of her lover's physical integrity, as far as it can be determined. Among certain classes man has *a priore* woman's indisputable guarantee that she is physically clean, owing, if to nothing else, to the restrictions thrown around her by society. If he doubts, let him ask for the same proof, and the woman will either cast him off altogether in her indignation, or furnish medical evidence to match his own. I doubt if the woman will be the one to hold back when this remedy for the social evil is proposed. Once teach her the need, moreover, and the demand will be made and insisted upon. Lincoln was right when he asserted that this is the duty of the father and mother. They have refused to assume the obligation, and the woman should now act for herself. Let us now turn to the man.

There is little or no hope, I confidently believe,

in legislation, or in restriction of any kind, which punishes the female offender and permits the male to go free. If the law is invoked let it be with a view to making every case of venereal disease reportable and isolable, as in the case of measles, scarlet fever, tuberculosis, and other less dangerous diseases. Moreover, let us now raise the embargo which we have placed upon the house of ill fame and the prostitute, and let us apprehend every man who is seen entering such a building, or encouraging advances from women on the street. Destroy the patronage and the revenue of these foci of evil and you sap their vitality forever, and in a much surer manner than by apprehending the object of man's deliberate search. You cannot deprive him of his ability to sin except by apprehending his person, not that of the woman whom he desires. If necessary seize both and establish a like penalty for the unfortunate woman and the criminal male. If the public really intends that this means shall prove successful it will defy failure. One organization in Philadelphia (The Christian League) claims to have extinguished, not scattered, a whole district of crime. But their work is not half done, for the men have all gone free. They state that " more than 3,000 complaints concerning disorderly houses, street walking and solicitation, obscene pictures, literature, entertainments and advertisements, speak-easies, gambling dens, fortune telling, robbery, abuse of children, etc., etc., have been received by us, and the great majority removed or abated." In the same report they state that there is now " no such circus of evil in this city (Philadelphia) to attract the boys."

These friends of ours have partly succeeded, but in one respect they accomplished the opposite of their intention. That crime center has settled elsewhere as surely as it was driven from its original site. Either in this city or in some other more favorably inclined, that colony (or many new ones) still lives its old life, and exerts its old influence on the men whom their families allow to slip away. The only real change is a multiplication into as many colonies as there were individuals before.

And what have they done with the men and boys whom they found guilty? Not a word of rebuke or of punishment has been meted out to them for their share in the mischief unless in the form of some well deserved bodily ailment; and even in such an event the worst punishment is likely to fall upon their innocent families and upon those with whom they come in daily contact. America prides herself in her women, and in the courteous bearing of her sons toward the feminine sex. Woman, we are fond of saying, is in this country granted the first place in our affections and honor. Is this not partly a myth, may I ask, when in many sections of the same country her virtue is bartered as an article of immoral commerce, and when the sale is discovered she alone is imprisoned or fined, while the man goes quietly home to his mother, wife, or children, perhaps all three, until a more convenient day?

Your mistake and mine will in all likelihood consist in extending our line of attack too far, and in attempting to concentrate on more than one objective. We have had a valuable lesson in the

Japanese war demonstrating the value of a clearly defined purpose, and of hammering at it above
and below the ground until success is won. There
is more at stake now than a city, even more than
a nation's independence. America's honor is in
the balance, has been for many a year, and more
awfully true is the fact that the fluctuation, of that
balance depends largely upon you and me. I believe that we can educate our boys and girls in
such a way as to protect them from evil until they
are men and women. Then by organized effort,
from Maine to California, invoke the law to punish the men and make public their crime, and you
will have gone far toward righting the burning
wrong which has bid fair to end in a conflagra-
tion. There will be no further need for Coventry
Patmore to quaintly sing —

> Who is the happy husband? He
> Who, scanning his unwedded life,
> Thanks Heaven with a conscience free
> 'Twas faithful to his future wife.

And now a practical word of advice which you
may never hear unless given by me at this time.

The laity have learned to look upon the attack which clergymen make at intervals upon questions of moral ethics as occasional necessary ebullitions, brief, fitful geyser-spoutings, which when once emitted subside and leave a lazy quiet, and the same conditions, behind. Especially those who are themselves offending against the laws of order and propriety delight in saying that " the clergy-man loses his head when he enters the lists for social reform." Perhaps there has been some foundation for the charge. If so, it has been due to ignorance on his part regarding the amount and efficiency of the ammunition and ordnance at his command. There is every reason for him to plan intelligently and confidently for the winning of the young boy and the future citizen, and, through him, for the purity of the American pop-ulace. The feeling that the clergyman's zeal will soon burn itself out should never be justified in this important crisis, and it is with the most genu-ine invitation that you shall take the lead in the task of educating our fathers, and mothers, and boys, and girls, that a physician is now addressing you. If the laity expect you to sermonize against the evil of the home and of the street, and then gradually retire from view and hearing, it is because they have seen this very thing occur from time immemorial. The task cannot be accomplished from the pulpit alone. The little must not be sacrificed in the attempt to gain much. Line upon line must be the order of the day. The enemy know that we are busy in many other interests. They have no other absorbing zeal. With them it is a matter of twenty-four hours out of the twenty-four, as against a half-hour spent weekly in the pulpit over reform. The thoroughness of the methods of the wayward outlasts and outvies the sudden brief outburst of virtue. Do not waste your time on the white slave traffic as reported by the newspapers. The prostitutes will laugh at you when you ask them if they are forcibly detained or compelled to live a life of shame. Instead, see that your own children are kept pure. See also that there is someone at the docks of the great immigrant steamship lines to guard from approach the young girls who are newly in this land, and see that they are cared for if they find, as is not infrequently the case, that they have been imported to fill the decimating ranks of prostitution. They need never reach such a life if you are there to greet them. Then there will be no white slave traffic. Even now it exists only in this first measure, and no woman need remain in a low resort longer than she deems advisable. On the other hand, you now know that there are thousands of deliberate prostitutes who would not and cannot (speaking from the standpoint of physical bondage) discard their natures. There are thousands more who can hardly earn a livelihood, humanly speaking, without the earnings of immorality, which fall so easily for a brief moment from pleasure's cornucopia.

Again let me advise you to make no such mistake as was made by the ministers in my city when all denominations met and prayed aloud over what they deemed a corrupt administration, and especially over our now honored mayor.

What is needed is an earnest petition sent up from the secret closet; then organization, persistent and relentless, through the breadth of our land, until the men, not the women, are driven from the streets and the houses. The women will then follow into the daylight for pure food and air. I believe that God must often turn His face aside in pity at our methods of working. Certainly it must be so when our desire for the removal of evil burns brightly for a day, and slumbers for a decade. He must look upon our purpose as shallow, and consider that our faith has run high and dry upon the rocks of difficulty, instead of venturing boldly forth upon the boundless ocean of Divine Providence.

Political influence is often around, in and behind immorality, and immorality has formed one of the means of support of political activity. But it need not be so one day longer than the serious portion of our people require to decree that a change shall, not should, come. There is a sufficient army of church members even, loyal and constant enough in other matters, to decide this battle in due time as it should be decided; but such disorganization of forces and such incompatibility of ideas and judgment have prevailed that an amalgamation of interests has been altogether impossible. As well bring match and gunpowder together and expect an absence of reaction as to expect political influences of the type that obtains in many of our American centres, to co-operate with the disinterested portion of the community in the suppression of the social evil. Our first object must be, therefore, education in the cause and effect of this long standing blight upon the healthy growth of our young man- and womanhood, since it would appear to be the only solution of a heretofore unsolved and very abstruse problem. We have tried and failed in the century-old method of rendering the crime too difficult to perform. Both the principle and the manner of execution were bad, and the failure should point the way to a more rational line of treatment. Convince the 14,000,000 boys and young men in the United States that prostitution and the divorce are kindred evils conspiring cheek and jowl to undermine the home life and purity of the American citizen, and you will win an invincible army for a vital cause. The women will assist you in winning the men, and should the latter refuse (which they will not do) Joan of Arc will succeed alone where the Generals have failed. Mark every man who cries aloud that the social evil is inevitable as one whose moral tension is at a low ebb.

My closing suggestion to the non-medical public, of which the clergyman and pastor must ever be the leader, is the following very homely illustration. You have learned quite recently that the best method of cure of tuberculosis is found neither in medicine, nor in open air, nor in overfeeding, nor in whiskey, once thought to be a specific for the disease. It consists in educating the body, and especially its weakened portions, gradually to withstand and conquer disease, by the judicious use of all natural methods and means. Thus we train nature's forces to successfully prosecute a work which has previously failed. In the same manner we have around, and in, and part of us, a diseased, but still young body politic, not the least of whose ailments is the social evil. The same method of attack is necessary and the same will succeed. Free open-air exposure of the wrong with its consequences to man, woman, and child, begun early, and earnestly taught by mother, father, physician, and pastor, will nourish the oncoming generation out of a dwarfed and deformed semi-morality, into a full and healthy manhood and womanhood, with shoulders thrown back and chest expanded with the sense of honest, round dealing by all mankind. It not only will be accomplished, but some of us will assist in the doing. Dr. Judson toiled at his post for six years before he won his first convert. At the end of the third year he was asked what evidence he saw of final success. "As much," he answered, "as that there is a God who will fulfil all His promises."

Dr. Judson had both grit and enthusiasm, and the necessary, unconquerable faith. I like to turn in the midst of a long, discouraging, but possible task — and all right tasks are possible — to the inspiring thought of one who died just as he began to accomplish:

> "This I beheld, or dreamed it in a dream;
> There spread a cloud of dust along a plain;
> And underneath the cloud, or in it, raged
> A furious battle, and men yelled, and swords
> Shocked upon swords and shields. A prince's banner
> Wavered, then staggered backward, hemmed by foes.
> A craven hung along the battle's edge,
> And thought, "Had I a sword of keener steel —
> That blue blade that the king's son bears — but this
> Blunt thing — !" He snapt and flung it from his hand,
> And lowering crept away, and left the field.
> Then came the king's son, wounded, sore bestead,
> And weaponless, he saw the broken sword,
> Hilt-buried in the dry and trodden sand,
> And ran and snatched it, and with battle shout,
> Lifted afresh, he hewed his enemy down,
> And saved a great cause that heroic day."